Ethical Decision Making
in
Everyday Work
Situations

Recent Titles from Quorum Books

Global Corporate Intelligence: Opportunities, Technologies, and Threats in the 1990s
George S. Roukis, Hugh Conway, and Bruce Charnov, editors

The Process of Change in American Banking: Political Economy and the Public Purpose
Jeremy F. Taylor

Drop Shipping as a Marketing Function: A Handbook of Methods and Policies
Nicholas T. Scheel

Manufacturing for the Security of the United States: Reviving Competitiveness and Reducing Deficits
Robert E. McGarrah

Employee Complaint Handling: Tested Techniques for Human Resource Managers
D. Keith Denton and Charles Boyd

Alcohol Problem Intervention in the Workplace: Employee Assistance Programs and Strategic Alternatives
Paul M. Roman, editor

Problem Employee Management: Proactive Strategies for Human Resource Managers
Willa M. Bruce

Electronic Data Interchange in Finance and Accounting
Robert J. Thierauf

Accounting Ethics: A Practical Guide for Professionals
Philip G. Cottell, Jr., and Terry M. Perlin

Privatization and Deregulation in Global Perspective
Dennis J. Gayle and Jonathan N. Goodrich, editors

The Deregulation of the World Financial Markets: Myths, Realities, and Impact
Sarkis J. Khoury

Social Change Philanthropy in America
Alan Rabinowitz

Ethical Decision Making
in
Everyday Work
Situations

MARY E. GUY

Q

QUORUM BOOKS

New York • Westport, Connecticut • London

Library of Congress Cataloging-in-Publication Data

Guy, Mary E.
    Ethical decision making in everyday work situations / Mary E. Guy.
      p.   cm.
    Includes bibliographical references.
    ISBN 0–89930–418–4 (lib. bdg. : alk. paper)
    1. Business ethics.   2. Decision-making—Moral and ethical
aspects. I. Title.
    HF5387.G89   1990
    174′.4—dc20   89–24348

British Library Cataloguing in Publication Data is available.

Library of Congress Catalog Card Number: 89–24348
ISBN: 0–89930–418–4

First published in 1990 by Quorum Books

Greenwood Press, Inc.
88 Post Road West, Westport, Connecticut   06881

Printed in the United States of America

The paper used in this book complies with the
Permanent Paper Standard issued by the National
Information Standards Organization (Z39.48–1984).

10 9 8 7 6 5 4 3 2 1

Dedicated to
those
who have the courage
to
make tough choices

Contents

Cases

Illustrations

TABLES

FIGURES

Preface

Making ethical decisions is easier said than done. Few people intentionally set out to be unethical. Yet often day-to-day activities lead people to succumb to expedient decisions which have less than ethical consequences. Many practical pressures make it difficult to perceive or adequately consider the ethical implications of conduct. By necessity, competent, successful managers must plant their feet firmly in the practical world of compromise and expediency. This book is written to help managers learn to practice, as well as to promote, ethical *and* expedient decision making in their work.

The 1980s brought to light an egregious disregard for ethics at the highest levels of government and business. In the wake of the arms-for-hostages deal between the United States and Iran, scandals within the U.S. Department of Housing and Urban Development, procurement deals between arms manufacturers and the Pentagon, insider trading on Wall Street, the forced resignation of House Speaker Jim Wright, and a plethora of leveraged buyouts, comes a renewed emphasis on the need to be sensitive to ethical concerns.

Although there are many conflict-of-interest laws, corporate policy statements, and administrative regulations that direct choices in the workplace, these are only briefly alluded to in this book. This is because laws, policies, regulations, and other forms of rules are external controls and, being so, it is fairly easy to make personnel aware of them. This book covers the exceptions to the rule, either because the problem under consideration is too unique or complex to be covered, or too routine to warrant a regulation. In other words, this book is about judgment.

The chapters that follow focus on actual situations and explain how ethical considerations come into play. Organizations shape a person's view of work-related situations. One's characteristic habits for relating to peers, customers, suppliers, clients, superiors, and subordinates are a blend of personal style, ethical choices, and organizational norms. To separate the discussion of ethics from the discussion of organizational behavior is to ignore the very important interaction between the employee and the company.

Some of the most common ethical dilemmas emanate from hierarchical relationships that produce a clash between administrative routines and professional, personal, or democratic values. Should a secretary keep quiet when a supervisor adds personal expenses to business-expense reimbursement claims? Should a salesperson push an inferior product just to meet a quota? Day-to-day decisions highlight the fact that even apparently routine decisions about budgeting and financial issues, personnel procedures, marketing strategies, supervisory styles, and reporting functions involve ethical issues and consequences.

Cost/benefit ratios, hierarchical chains of command, assembly lines, and budgets do not have to give way in order to ensure ethical decisions. Decision makers need to be aware, though, of the ethical considerations that are involved. There are always ethical implications to decisions about how to calculate costs and benefits, how to organize a work force, how to monitor assembly line production, and how to allocate resources.

Many people deal with ethical issues every day even though they do not realize it. Ethics is not a weighty subject restricted to the province of high-minded philosophical debates. Ethics is an everyday application of a standard of relating to others. Ethical considerations are called into play when an employer is asked to provide a reference on an employee who is known to have a drinking problem or an attendance problem, or any other counterproductive work habit. If the person providing the reference withholds information, the next employer is misled as to the new employee's work habits. If the person providing the reference gives the information, the employee's right to privacy is violated. A balancing act must be mastered between the competing values of honesty, promise keeping, integrity, and loyalty.

This book attempts to bring the philosophical discussion of ethics down to earth and show the reader how to use personal judgment to make ethical decisions. It is neither a book about philosophy nor a book about decision making. Other authors have already covered both those domains far better than I. My contribution is to meld philosophy with decision making and translate from the esoteric literature to the reader who wants a commonsense approach to making ethical decisions. This book targets the interface of decision making and ethics, showing the considerations that must be brought to bear for a decision to be an ethical one. It merges the philosophy of ethics with the management science of decision making and applies the result to daily decision problems confronting managers.

By no means is this work to be a preaching to the reader. Neither I, nor anyone else I know, has a pipeline to the Truth (at least one that is acceptable to enough people to make it worth printing). Rather, the book sets forth the topic under consideration, shows the values that relate to it, presents alternative solutions, explains their consequences if adopted, and then examines the ethical implications of each alternative.

Chapter 1 is an introduction to the subject matter, showing how daily decisions are based on each person's values, whether or not the decision maker is aware of this fact. Ethics is defined and the relationship between ethical behavior and morality is clarified. The definition is followed with a discussion of what "ethics" is about, and why it is important to be sensitive to the ethical dimension of work-related decisions. Ten guiding values that serve as the foundation for ethical decisions are explored: caring, honesty, accountability, promise keeping, pursuit of excellence, loyalty, fairness, integrity, respect for others, and responsible citizenship.

Chapter 2 focuses on decision making. Differences in people's preferences result from differences in their priorities. And priorities are based on values. For this reason, it is impossible for complex decision making to be value neutral. A rational decision is one that maximizes a value, which may be efficiency, efficacy, reliability, controllability, marketability, or any of many other values. At the root of any of these are basic assumptions about the importance of accountability, pursuit of excellence, and responsible citizenship. Promoting one alternative over another involves trading off one value for another.

Many people are expressing a renewed interest in intuitive decision making as an adjunct to rational decision making. Right-brain thinking involves the decision maker's accepting subliminal cues as acceptable data in addition to facts and figures. Both rational and intuitive decision making can be appropriate for approaching a decision problem. These, or any other models of decision making, are based on a conglomeration of values held by the individual decision maker. Chapter 2 closes with a definition of *ethical* decision making and an example of a decision problem to show how ethical calculations enter the picture.

Chapters 3, 4, 5, and 6 break ethical decision making into four categories: those that involve interpersonal relationships, those that involve differentiating between personal gain and loyalty to one's employer, those that involve getting along in the context of company norms, and those that involve good citizenship in the organization as well as in the community. The cases presented in these chapters take a proactive approach to ethical inquiry by presenting situations, teasing out the ethical issues that are involved, and applying various scenarios for reaching an ethical decision. The situations demonstrate the tension that exists between ethical decision making, coping with daily exigencies, and accommodating the preferences of stakeholders. Each case depicts ordinary circumstances that personnel often encounter. The relevant values in each case are identified and alternative solutions are explored.

Chapter 7 summarizes the relationship between ethics and decision making and gives a prescription for ensuring ethical decision making. The book closes by emphasizing that the best position executives can be in is one that promotes ethical decision making and the behavior that follows, rather than one that results in the predicament of having to put out fires caused by someone's failure to realize the ethical dimensions to a problem.

Acknowledgments

The development of this book would not have been possible without hours of thoughtful discussion afforded to me by scores of employees, ranging in rank from chief executive officers to vice presidents, to midlevel managers, to supervisors, to line personnel. They have been employed or have served in a variety of organizations, ranging from federal, state, and local agencies; to large corporations and small entrepreneurial firms; to banks and utility companies; to universities and schools; and to not-for-profit commissions and boards. To all of you, your insights have been invaluable, and I thank you for the opportunities you have given me to walk beside you as you struggled to choose the right answers to your dilemmas.

My able research asssistants, Sara Bradley and Rita Macon, devoted many hours to researching materials and handling the technical aspects of producing this manuscript. I extend to them my warmest wishes for their budding careers, and trust that the right solutions will come easily.

I am grateful to my teachers, disguised as my students, who have wrangled with me and with one another as we explored the nuances to ethical decision making. Some of their own experiences are included as cases in the chapters of this book. The names have been changed in most instances, as have the details of the circumstances, in order to protect the confidentiality of everyone involved.

I owe special words of thanks to Cindy Michelson, Alva Brownfield,

Reata Busby, Harris Cornett, Norma Ann Dodd, John Donohue, Jay Glass, Daphine Jackson, Donna Miranda, Brenda Lee Rice, Patricia Todd, Cecil Usher, and Lynne Windham. And last, but by no means least, I thank Eric Valentine for his editorial insight and helpful suggestions in the preparation of this manuscript.

Part I

Introduction to Ethics and Decision Making

1

Values, Ethics, and Personal Responsibility

An inclination is where virtue must begin, and no one need despair because, say, his courage lags behind his temperance. Just being aware of it is a sign of a desire to do something about it, though no one should expect total conversion overnight. For no less than in any other human endeavor, in our quest for moral virtues the law of progress is one of gradual perfection.

—Yves Simon

The search for excellence begins with ethics. Every time a person chooses between alternatives, the choice is based on assumptions that lie at the heart of a moral code. The code is grounded in values that provide the framework for principled reasoning and ethical decisions.

Commerce depends for its very existence on the ethical behavior of the vast majority of participants. It requires that contracts are honored, private property is respected, and promises are kept. It relies upon the unspoken sentiments of fair play and camaraderie. Ethical practices make good business sense, because ethical companies suffer less resentment, less litigation, and less regulatory oversight (Solomon and Hanson, 1985). Furthermore, ethical managers and ethical businesses tend to be more trusted and better treated by employees, suppliers, stockholders, and consumers.

Organizations are a reflection of society; they are the method by which individuals unite to form a network of common interest. And each organization is a fluid enterprise. At its center are the managers and executives responsible for directing the resources of the company. Shareholders own the capital and expect a return on their investment. Workers produce the goods and expect a decent wage and safe working conditions. To have a successful enterprise, each group must be responsive to the others and balance its interest against the interests of the others. When the balance is upset or when the interests pull too hard against each other, the ethical system is damaged. For an enterprise to continually give value to human effort and to encourage creative achievements, a balance of all interests is required (Parry, 1985).

Administrative actions are shaped by three domains: legality, free choice, and integrity (Mueller, 1977). The law defines and constrains the limits of potential actions, specifying the bounds of lawful behavior. What is legal is not necessarily moral; what is not prohibited by law is not necessarily ethical; and what minimally meets the law is not necessarily proper. While the law codifies customs, ideals, beliefs, and moral values of a society, it cannot possibly cover all possible human actions.

Free choice represents complete freedom of personal choice to do anything one desires. But, paraphrasing Justice Oliver Wendell Holmes, the right to swing your fist stops where the other person's nose begins. In other words, people have a right to do whatever they want as long as their actions do not negatively affect others. Ethical behavior is more constrained than this, however. Ethical behavior is that behavior which is the *right* thing to do, given the circumstances.

The rightness of actions is constrained by the third domain, integrity, which is obedience to the unenforceable. This represents unwritten, often unspoken, guidelines for behavior for which no legal mandates or prohibitions exist. It is the grey area where neither law nor free choice prevail. This is the realm of integrity, the necessary foundation for ethical decision making.

Ethics is different from law because it involves no formal sanctions. It is different from etiquette because it goes beyond mere social convention. It is different from religion because it makes no theological assumptions. It is different from aesthetics because it is aimed at conduct and character rather than objects. It is different from prudence because it goes beyond self-interest to include the interests of others. It is different from finance and marketing and governing and parenting and carpentry, in that it does not involve a special purpose or special role as its point of departure. Ethics is both a process of inquiry and a code of conduct. Ethical inquiry consists of asking the questions of what is good and what is evil, what is right and what is wrong. As a code of conduct, it is a sort of inner eye that enables people to see the rightness or wrongness of their actions.

RELATIONSHIP BETWEEN VALUES, ETHICS, AND MORALS

Values are core beliefs about what is intrinsically desirable. They underly the choices made in work decisions just as they underlie the choices made in one's private life. They give rise to ideals that are called *ethics* or *morals*. The two terms are sometimes confused. Actually, *ethics* and *morals* are synonymous. While *ethics* is derived from Greek, *morals* is derived from Latin. They are interchangeable terms referring to ideals of character and conduct. These ideals, in the form of codes of conduct, furnish criteria for distinguishing between right and wrong.

Ethical inquiry requires the decision maker to consider facts in light of important values. The conclusions reached are often stated as judgments, such as "he is a good person"; "bribery is wrong, even though it may be profitable"; "caring about others is the essence of virtue"; "the act was irresponsible"; "her character, and the character of her firm, is admirable"; or, "the key to doing right by Jones is doing what is for his own good." This is to say that moral judgments and problems are couched in a certain kind of language. Terms like *good, bad, right, wrong, obligation, duty, ought, should, rights*, and *virtue* are the characteristic coinage of moral discourse and invoke a moral frame of reference.

Contradictory values contribute to the complexity of ethical inquiry. To maximize one value often requires diminishing others. For example, while an organization's dedication to producing quality products or services is laudable, an emphasis on quality may deemphasize quantity, or in some circumstances, efficiency. Or, while objectivity and impersonal procedures and actions are seen as good, they preclude taking individual circumstances into account. Or, while friendship on the job is good, in some cases it makes it more difficult to promote other important values, such as efficiency or fairness.

Everyone who makes decisions relies on a moral code, shifting though it may be. Decision makers may be only partially sensitive to the cross-cutting loyalties, interests, and preconceptions that actually shape their choices. Individual thoughtfulness is the key to ethical decision making. A moral code must be conscientiously applied to the issue at hand such that any decision maximizes the most important values and minimizes the less important values.

A corporation is made up of individual employees. When they go to work each day they take their respective moral codes with them. To a great extent, it is true that to have ethical employees, a company must hire ethical applicants. But there is no guarantee that people with high scores on a test of moral values will necessarily behave ethically. Knowing what is right and good is one thing, but what really matters is whether or not people put their values into practice in the workplace.

Ethics refers to standards by which individuals evaluate their own conduct and the conduct of others. Most ethical decisions do not hold one's life in the balance. They are day-to-day decisions that people make and often take for granted in the world of work: treating others with respect, keeping promises, making personnel decisions, looking out for friends, giving and accepting gifts, padding expense vouchers, or reporting wrongdoing. On a greater scale of wrongdoing are failure to respect confidential information, failure to report important information, invasions of privacy, unnecessary secrecy, conflicts of interest, kickbacks, taking advantage of insider information, theft of company funds, bribery, and commercial espionage.

Employees engage in some behaviors because they assume that as long as they are the only persons doing it, little harm can come of it. Ethical problems mushroom when several people follow the same logic. Before long, what started as inattentiveness to complaints, failure to evaluate inefficiency and waste, and failure to keep abreast of what is going on in the company results in secrecy, doing less than the best, corruption, and ultimately ineffectiveness.

Being sensitive to ethical issues and incorporating them into decision making decreases the likelihood of costly mistakes. Ethical wrongdoing affects morale within the company and has the potential to damage relations with the company's major constituents, including customers, clients, shareholders, and suppliers, as well as the general public. The way executives handle sticky issues can fundamentally alter their effectiveness and credibility because their decisions reflect their personal integrity and courage, influence the trust others are willing to place in them, and communicate conviction or vacillation on issues that matter deeply to many others. Some corporations create a moral environment by specifying a distinct set of values and standards to which they hold their people accountable. A corporation that is serious about maintaining high ethical standards may shut down a plant when it fails to meet internal quality standards, remove controversial products from the market, and fire individuals who cross ethical lines.

Unethical acts are usually not so much a product of greed or immorality as they are of ethical naïveté. Unwitting employees may have done what they were told to do and, in the process, become scapegoats for someone else's indiscretion. A midlevel manager, pressed from above, may mistakenly believe that in business, you do whatever you have to do to survive. When upper management is not clear about standards, priorities, or limits, the manager is left to his or her assumptions about what actions to take. Or, employees hidden in the anonymity of a large organization think that their actions will remain undiscovered regardless of the rightness or wrongness of their behavior.

Employment involves an exchange relationship between people. Employees exchange their time and effort not only for the job and the salary but also for all the position brings: career; self-esteem; and the quality of life defined with and by other people in terms of respect, status, recognition, admiration, and friendship. The good life is not only what money can buy, but what relationships and rewards are gained from one's daily activities.

ACTIONS SPEAK LOUDER THAN WORDS

In ethics, actions speak louder than words. While codes of ethics may be public relations niceties, they do not adequately stem unethical behavior in business and government. Ethical behavior on the job means staying close to peers, subordinates, superiors, and customers, and retaining a realistic view of what is good and just in the world. Ethical behavior on the job is not separable from that in other parts of people's lives.

No organization is a moral sanctuary, absolved of moral responsibility. Institutions are created by people to serve people's ends (Anderson, 1954).

Unwritten but tacitly understood codes of conduct that are taken for granted in small, family-owned businesses are not as effective in large, impersonal organizations. Although the same rules may apply in large organizations as in small businesses, they often disappear in the anonymity. The personal touch and informal controls that are as meaningful in a small shop as they are in a family become vague, if not lost, in vast, impersonal bureaucracies. This does not absolve large corporations and agencies of ethical responsibilities, however. Organizations are not like machines that have no thinking parts. The means and ends of any organization do not come out of thin air, nor once adopted are they fixed in stone. They are formulated by people and can be modified by people.

In 1986, the U.S. Bureau of Justice reported that, in federal cases alone, almost eleven thousand people were convicted and sentenced for fraud, forgery, and embezzlement. In that same year, the U.S. Chamber of Commerce estimated loss due to white-collar crime to be between twenty billion and forty billion dollars (*Lippman Report*, 1987). The total loss is far greater, however. What cannot be measured by numbers is the loss of trust between government and business leaders in the flurry of dishonest activity.

The growing cohort of middle-aged and older participants in the work force has become noticeably impatient with ethical breaches. Respondents to a survey conducted in the mid–1980s were asked to rate the following crimes: falsifying an income tax return, cheating on an exam, accepting money for their vote in an election, and setting a vacant building on fire that an owner cannot rent in order to collect insurance (Wright, 1985). When categorized by age, it was clear that older subjects, those ages 36–66, had recorded a significantly higher aversion to unethical practices than did younger respondents, ages 22–35. Unfortunately, it is impossible to tell whether older respondents had become less tolerant of ethical violations as they matured or whether they were always less tolerant than younger respondents.

The lead story in a 1987 issue of *Crain's Chicago Business* included the report of a survey of 452 readers who had responded to a survey on business ethics (Hornung, 1987). Bribery, kickbacks, payoffs, deception, and lying were frequently mentioned among the standard busi-

Table 1.1
Survey of Business Ethics

Question	Yes	No
Generally speaking, good ethics is good business.	99%	1%
Are most corporate executives honest?	82%	18%
In your industry are there practices that you consider unethical?	73%	27%
Does the rhetoric of business ethics exceed the reality for most companies?	73%	27%
Should business schools make courses in business ethics available to all business students?	05%	5%
Should ethics of the business world be different from personal ethics?	11%	89%
Should companies provide employees with training on the ethical standards of the company and the repercussions for violations?	93%	7%

ness practices that respondents wished to see eliminated in their industries. Table 1.1 presents a summary of the responses.

When respondents were asked how their ethics compared with those of their peers, only 1 percent said their ethics were lower, 20 percent said their ethics were about the same, 53 percent said their ethics were higher, and 26 percent said their ethics were much higher. In other words, over three-fourths of the respondents rated their ethics as being higher than those of their peers (Hornung, 1987, p. 63).

The report evokes the notion that competitive pressures force perfectly decent people to act unethically. The dissonance between how people would like to act and how they actually act is reflected in this disparity. When corporate executives are making decisions, 82 percent of the respondents said that they ought to weigh claims of corporate constituencies other than shareholders. This includes those with competing interests, such as labor, consumer, and community groups (Hornung, 1987). Only one-third of all respondents said their company had a formal procedure other than the ordinary chain of command for employees to make complaints about such things as hazardous or unfair company practices.

Crain's also asked its readers to list the most difficult ethical dilemmas they had confronted in their business activities. Respondents listed a number of incidents, including the following:

- One person received an order from his general manager to falsify year-end financial information. The preliminary figures were nowhere near budget. He refused to do it and was fired.

- The president of the company where one respondent worked had asked her to issue false progress billings to a customer.

- A respondent had to decide whether to fire two people for falsifying time reports. It was such a common thing in her business that the employees were shocked that she took the falsification seriously.

- One respondent felt ethically bound to report accurate information to a client even though his company had ordered him not to do so.

- A respondent's advertising firm was unwilling to meet the gift giving of the competition. The firm lost a major corporate account because five marketing managers from the client firm sent them a list of gifts they wanted for Christmas. One even listed a color television. The advertising firm told the marketing managers to forget it, and lost the account because of their refusal not to "play the game."

When asked to list the worst ethical dilemmas facing business, here is what Chicago respondents said: fair treatment of all employees; cheating to get ahead; under-the-table deals; kickbacks; payoffs; government corruption; being driven by self-interest; trying to improve the bottom line, no matter how; and a lack of ethical leadership at the top (Hornung, 1987). These problems are not unique to the Chicago area. The drive for short-term profits is a threat to American business ethics. When next quarter's bottom line outweighs all other considerations, ethical short-cuts are the inevitable result.

Government as well as business has been grappling with ethical dilemmas. Public administration issued a call twenty years ago for more attention to be paid to the values that serve as the foundation for government action (Marini, 1971). But as we head toward the twenty-first century, there is a suspicion that money has replaced intelligence and hard work as the way to get things done. Some even say that Washington's atmosphere during the 1980s was reminiscent of what city halls must have been like in the days of Boss Tweed, but in the 1980s the bagmen had fancy college degrees and five-hundred-dollar suits. Government as well as business had gone beyond the bounds of individual conscience and common sense.

BUSINESS VERSUS GOVERNMENT ETHICS

Ethical decision making is as important, if not more important, in public agencies as it is in private companies. Some writers treat business and public agencies as two different enterprises so unrelated as to be incomparable. Such a dichotomy between public and private organizations artificially divides organizations and the discussion of what goes on within them. Barry Bozeman (1987) argues that there are two fundamental sources of authority upon which all organizations are based: economic authority and political authority, each of which exists as a unique dimension. Bozeman argues that it is the authority mix that has a pervasive influence on the organization as a whole, its constraints, and its operations, not the mere fact of whether the organization is chartered by government or private enterprise. So, rather than being wholly public or private, organizations are more or less public or private. As the argument goes, organizations may be more public in some respects and more private in other respects. Thus, an organization lies somewhere on a publicness dimension. Whether or not you accept Bozeman's argument, at least it should be obvious that human behavior is much the same whether people are working in a government agency, a not-for-profit agency, or a for-profit business. At the heart of the enterprise, whether it is business, government, or not-for-profit, there must be a guiding philosophy that generates a fundamental set of beliefs or assumptions upon which to operate and to guide decisions.

PHILOSOPHICAL FOUNDATIONS OF ETHICS

Ethics has been a subject of systematic investigation for over twenty-five hundred years (Leys, 1968). From as far back as Plato's *Republic* to Immanuel Kant's eighteenth-century *Critique of Judgment* (Cornford, 1945) to John Rawls's twentieth-century *Theory of Justice*, philosophers have struggled with defining what is right and good and just. Kant and Plato were concerned with the same problems even though they did not uphold the same ideals. ''Kant, for example, disapproved of absolute governments, and he declared that lying is never justified; Plato on the other hand, longed for a benevolent dictatorship and defended what he called 'medicinal myths' '' (Leys, 1968, p. 70). Both philosophers were aspiring to consistency in conduct, and each in his own way was reaching for that community of attitudes that makes rational discussion possible.

Kant justified doing the morally right thing by invoking the ''categorical imperative,'' meaning a universal unconditional obligation (Paton, 1947). Kant's categorical imperative is that ''one ought never to act except in such a way that one can also will that one's maxim should become a universal law'' (Beauchamp and Bowie, 1979, p. 20). This means that people should behave in such a manner that if everyone else acted the same way, everyone would benefit. Put in everyday language, this means that making promises with the intention of breaking them when they no longer suit the promisor's purposes is to disobey the categorical imperative. More recently the contemporary philosopher John Rawls focused on the best way to achieve equal amounts of liberty for everyone and, in the face of inevitable inequalities, sought a principle which would maximize the condition of the least advantaged. His work focuses on the distribution of justice to achieve this end.

Philosophical approaches that seek universal truths, such as those discussed by Plato, Kant, and Rawls, are deontological. A functional code of ethics usually draws from two philosophical frameworks, one deontological and one teleological. Deontology is a view that holds that there are universal rules that serve as moral guides, such as those put forth by Plato, Kant, and Rawls. A deontological approach to ethics maintains that the concept of duty is independent of the concept of good. That is, acts have significance regardless of whether or not good comes of them. A belief in obligations, such as promise keeping and keeping contracts, for example, is a deontological notion that someone should do something because they said they would, regardless of whether a good is associated with it.

A teleological approach to ethics is utilitarian. It assumes that the moral worth of actions is determined solely by the consequences of the actions. Utility refers to social happiness, based on the states of mind of the individuals involved. The principle of utility is an important part of American moral thinking. But because it is, it is not unusual to have simultaneously contradictory implications. What looks good from a personal, social, environmental, business, or religious point of view may not look good from another point of view. What looks right from a business perspective often looks wrong from a government perspective and vice versa. And what looks right from a personal point of view may look wrong from a business or governmental perspective.

There are three alternative routes to a teleological perspective. The first is *egoism*, which is pure self-interest. The second is *act utilitarianism*, which means actions are ethical when they produce pleasure. The third is *rule utilitarianism*, which means that generalizable codes of conduct can be established, but they are not universal.

Rule utilitarianism is sort of a bounded deontological approach in which there is an agreed-upon moral code, but that code is subject to ongoing revision rather than accepted as lasting or universal. For example, if confronted with the choice of giving fifty dollars to charity or to a friend, this approach dictates that the choice should be based on that which would lead to the best consequences for all affected, that is, the greatest good for the greatest number. In business, efficiency is a means to higher profits and to lower prices, so it is the greatest good for the greatest number. Likewise, in government, efficiency means being able to provide more services for the same tax dollars. Business is founded on a utilitarian conception of the good society (Beauchamp and Bowie, 1979). In the United States, government services are also grounded in a utilitarian concept but guided by the deontological notion of equality, freedom, and the right to property.

ADMINISTRATIVE ETHICS

The beauty and the challenge of ethics is that it provides a framework for decision making. Kathryn Denhardt (1988) captured this dilemma when she defined administrative ethics as a process of independently critiquing alternatives, based on core social values within the context of the organization, subject to personal and professional accountability.

There are three fundamental questions of ethics which require an unequivocal positive response (Baier, 1958):

• Should anyone do what is right when doing so is not to that person's advantage?
• Does anyone do what is right when doing so is not to that person's advantage?
• Can anyone know what is right?

Table 1.2
Ten Core Values

Caring	Loyalty
Honesty	Fairness
Accountability	Integrity
Promise Keeping	Respect for Others
Pursuit of Excellence	Responsible Citizenship

Answering "Yes" to these questions commits one to ethical inquiry and ethical decision making.

VALUES AS GUIDEPOSTS FOR ETHICAL DECISION MAKING

A general consensus has developed around ten essential values that are central to relations between people (Barry, 1979; Beauchamp and Bowie, 1979; Josephson, 1988; Solomon and Hanson, 1985). Although they overlap to some degree, they provide a means for judging interpersonal choices and behaviors. By evaluating how these values relate to an issue under consideration, and by analyzing who the stakeholders are in the decision, the ethical implications of an action become clearer. Table 1.2 lists them.

Caring means treating people as ends in themselves, not means to an end. It means having compassion, treating people courteously and with dignity, helping those in need, and avoiding harm to others.

The difficulty with this value in work settings is that organizations use people as ends by virtue of the employment contract. To an employer, an employee is both an end and a means to an end (productivity), so there is an inevitable trade-off. Working is an exchange relationship. Although the balance is fairly close to level, it is nevertheless an unequal relationship, with the employer having more weight than the employee. This principle also applies to colleagues who may be tempted to curry favor with someone not for the value of the relationship, but for the value of what that person can do to help them achieve their ends.

Honesty means being truthful and not deceiving or distorting. In the long run, there is usually less advantage and more harm to being dishonest than to being honest. One by one, deceptions undermine the capacity for open exchange and erode credibility. Individuals who lose their reputation for truthfulness usually cannot accomplish very much.

The people who want to be lied to nevertheless resent it when the lies are discovered. To prevent embarrassment, telling "little white lies" or "medicinal myths" as Plato called them, to oneself or one's friends is common. But privacy can be protected just as well by silence. Deception is always discoverable, and if it is about something interesting or someone important, it is more than likely to be discovered.

Indirect deceptions, such as withholding needed information from opponents or allowing misinterpretations of one's works to stand without correction may be as tempting as lies. But business is not the same as a poker game, where bluffing is part of the skill. Everyone involved in a poker game knows the rules. But business activity is not isolated from the rest of society. It is not something relegated to the back rooms of society, played for the amusement of a privileged few. Many nonbusiness people are involved with business activities, whether as customers, as neighbors sharing or competing for the same resources, or as citizens affected by large government contracts with business.

Accountability means accepting the consequences of one's actions and accepting the responsibility for one's decisions and their consequences. This means setting an example for others and avoiding even the appearance of impropriety. Asking such questions as How would this be interpreted if it appeared in the newspaper? or What sort of person would do such a thing? bring accountability dilemmas into focus.

Promise keeping means keeping one's commitments. When promises have been made, they are supported by the fact that the obligation to keep promises is among the most important of generally accepted obligations. To be worthy of trust, promises must be kept and commitments fulfilled. There are many stakeholders in organizational decisions, including employees, clients, shareholders, dealers, suppliers, unions, local communities, competitors, and customers. Promises and agreements to and among stakeholders create expectations of performance and establish obligations.

Pursuit of excellence means striving to be as good as one can be. It means being diligent, industrious, and committed. It means being well informed and well prepared. It is not enough to be content with mediocrity, but it is also not right to win "at any cost." Many companies explicitly state that the ends will not justify illegal means. Results are stressed, but so is the manner and the method of achievement. A sizeable number of firms stress that managers and top officials who know about misconduct and who either endorse it or avoid taking steps to correct the situation are liable in the same way as the offender.

Loyalty means being faithful and loyal to those with whom one has dealings. In a business context, this means safeguarding the ability to make independent professional judgments by scrupulously avoiding undue influence and conflicts of interest. Every organization is dependent upon cohesion and demands loyalty from its members. Loyalty becomes an institutional good. It is the oil that keeps an organization from grinding with dissension. But loyalty is not an unmitigated good. It depends upon to whom and for what purpose the loyalty is given. If loyalty means blind, unquestioning obedience, inevitably the values of the organization clash with broader social and political values. Blind obedience is thoughtless and does not prepare a decision maker to weigh values in question and make the best decision. For example, public relations professionals must walk a thin line between sometimes incompatible moral values of economic dealings, political activity, education issues, and environmental matters (Wright, 1985). A public relations expert cannot excel for long without having developed the skill to evaluate the values in question and develop a principled compromise.

Fairness means being open-minded, willing to admit error, and not overreaching or taking undue advantage of another's adversities, and it means avoiding arbitrary or capricious favoritism. It means treating people equally and making decisions based on notions of justice.

Integrity means using independent judgment and avoiding conflicts of interest, restraining from self-aggrandizement, and resisting economic pressure. It means being faithful to one's deepest beliefs, acting on one's conviction, and not adopting an end-justifies-the-means philosophy that ignores principle.

Examining the extent to which self-interest is present in a decision helps to clarify and resolve conflicts among obligations. Of course it is appropriate to consider one's personal needs, desires, and personal ambitions. The appropriateness is bounded by obligations, however. The proper place of one's own interests, whether or not in collision with one's duties, arises when choosing whether to accept, or impose, an obligation. It is generally agreed that moral reasons are superior to reasons of self-interest, reasons of long-range interest superior to reasons of short-range interest, and reasons of self-interest superior to caprice (Baier, 1958).

Respect for others means recognizing each person's right to privacy and self-determination and having respect for human dignity. It means being courteous, prompt, and decent, and providing others with information that they need to make informed decisions.

Responsible citizenship means that actions should be in accord with societal values. All high officials, whether in government or business, have some degree of discretion, and many have a great deal. Appropriate standards for the exercise of this discretion must be practiced. Within government, both legislative and executive judgment ought to reflect the will of the people in accord with democratic values. Public servants have a special obligation to lead by example, to safeguard and advance the integrity and reputation of the legislative process, and to avoid even the appearance of impropriety. John Rohr (1989) argues that career civil servants must base their ethical behavior in public administration on three regime values: equality, property, and freedom.

In both government and business it is important to obey just laws. If a law is unjust, it should be protested through accepted means. Democratic rights and privileges should be exercised by voting and expressing informed views. When in a position of leadership or authority, one must respect democratic processes of decision making.

These ten values are at the core of ethical standards that have survived the ages. They may be remembered by the acronym CHAPELFIRZ: *c*aring, *h*onesty, *a*ccountability, *p*romise keeping, pursuit of *e*xcellence, *l*oyalty, *f*airness, *i*ntegrity, *r*espect for others, and responsible citizenship. When put into practice, these values generate widely recognized virtues that provide benchmarks for ethical decision making. These virtues are, for example, moderation, order, resolution, industriousness, sincerity, and humility. Principles such as the following are based on various combinations of the ten core values and virtues that are generated by them:

Treat all human beings with fairness. This principle emphasizes the importance of fairness.

Do unto others as you would have them do unto you. This principle has been a prominent ethical force in Buddhism, ancient Greek philosophy, Hinduism, Judaism, and Christianity. It emphasizes caring, honesty, accountability, promise keeping, loyalty, fairness, integrity, and respect for others.

Act that your act will produce, over the long range, maximum good. For example, breaking a promise might be expedient in the present situation but greatly risks a bad reputation and consequent failure in the long term, and is therefore judged to be unethical. An ethical person must often forego short-time benefits for long-term advantages. This emphasizes accountability, promise keeping, pursuit of excellence, integrity, and responsible citizenship.

Act that your act could be made a general law that could be proved from human experience to work toward general human and social success. This emphasizes caring, honesty, accountability, pursuit of excellence, promise keeping, fairness, integrity, respect for others, and responsible citizenship. The question to ask related to this rule is, Would it still be ethical if everybody did this? For example, if stockbrokers were to sell poor-quality stocks, investors would soon stop using all stockbrokers. Therefore, promoting poor-quality stocks is wrong according to this rule. Consistency is within a moral code. This means not making exceptions of yourself that you are unwilling to make for others, such as breaking in line to buy movie tickets, cheating on exams, and giving kickbacks and bribes.

In addition to principles that guide ethical decisions, the notion of distributive justice also serves as a guide. There are alternative rules of distributive justice, meaning that one can apply different principles in different contexts. Five alternatives are:

1. to each person an equal share
2. to each person according to individual need
3. to each person according to individual effort
4. to each person according to societal contribution
5. to each person according to merit.

These rules maximize different values. The first maximizes fairness. The second maximizes caring for others. The third and fifth maximize the pursuit of excellence. The fourth maximizes responsible citizenship.

Another approach to codifying ethical decision making is to follow rules based on ethical premises:

Rule 1. Consider the well-being of others, including nonparticipants. This rule emphasizes caring and respect for others.

Rule 2. Think as a member of the community, not as an isolated individual. This emphasizes loyalty, integrity, respect for others, and responsible citizenship.

Rule 3. Obey, but do not depend solely on the law. This emphasizes integrity and responsible citizenship.

Rule 4. Ask, What sort of person would do such a thing? This emphasizes all the values by calling each into question.

Rule 5. Respect the customs of others, but not at the expense of your own ethics. This emphasizes accountability, fairness, integrity, and respect for others.

A decision maker should not proceed with the notion that there is one, and only one, right answer to an ethical dilemma. In most situations there will be several answers, perhaps each quite different from one another. The first task is to distinguish what values are at stake. The second task is to select alternatives that will maximize the important values. The third task is to select the best of the available alternatives. Some alternatives will be more ethical than others, or, among a set of equally ethical alternatives, some will be more consistent with one's personal goals and value system than others.

Foregoing one alternative for another means that some values are exchanged in favor of other, more important values. This leads to the importance of distinguishing between the principle of compromise and the compromise of principle. Compromise is frequently necessary, not only to find a common ground among decision makers, but to find one optimal alternative. But willingness to compromise in order to reach an agreeable, ethical solution is very different from a willingness to jettison ethics altogether in a compromise of principle.

Choices are not made directly between values, but rather between options that differ in the extent to which they embody particular values or in the emphasis some values receive in relation to others. Values shape the way problems are perceived. They are crucial to the realization that something is a problem to be solved rather than a condition to be accepted. And they are crucial to determining the focus of the problem. It is the task of ethical reasoning to discern ways of achieving decisions or of managing enduring conflict that will maximize the most important values while minimizing only those of less importance.

CODES OF ETHICS AND THE ROLE THEY PLAY IN WORK SETTINGS

An ethical code is a statement of aspirations and a code of commitment to stakeholders. A code of ethics should describe a standard of integrity and competence beyond that required by law—which is the bare minimum. Codes typically cover the highest ideals of caring, honesty, accountability, promise keeping, pursuit of excellence, loyalty, fairness, integrity, respect for others, and responsible citizenship as these values are applied to the work context, but they do so in general, sometimes vague terms. In short, they address the ten core values as applied to the work setting. They legitimate organizational values and may help provide guidance, especially if they involve implementation guidelines, such as the code of the International City Management Association, which adopted a code of ethics in 1924 and has updated it periodically since then (*Public Management*, 1987).

Codes of ethics are intended to help people make ethical decisions when there are no clear-cut right or wrong answers to guide them. There are standards of business practices often built into codes of ethics. These include statements warning against conflicts of interest and conflicts of obligation. Conflicts of obligation occur when people's principles or commitments demand that they fulfill two or more obligations simultaneously, though only one can be fulfilled at a time. Conflicts of interest occur when an individual has two or more interests such that if both are pursued, there may result an unjustified effect on one's work.

Codes of ethics make those who write them feel good—but they may do little else than spell out a few unequivocally forbidden behaviors. Chatov (1980) lists what he says are the fourteen most frequently prohibited employee behaviors regarding organizational activities: extortion, gifts, and kickbacks; conflict of interest; illegal political payments; violation of laws in general; use of insider information; bribery; falsification of corporate accounts; violation of antitrust laws; moonlighting; violation of secrecy agreements; ignorance of work-related laws; fraud and deception; and using ends to justify questionable means.

Even though codes may be honored in the breach more often than not, the absence of a written code says the organization has no coherent statement of what its ethical core is. Responses to a survey of 1,082 business leaders, business school deans, and members of Congress say the adoption of a corporate code of ethics is the most effective way to encourage ethical behavior. Respondents said the least effective was legislation (Andriacco, 1988).

Codes of ethics should be more than a negative statement of how to stay out of trouble (Rohr, 1989). Ethical statements should guide positive behavior. Lists of ethical no-nos promote an office-boy mentality that is destructive of the self-respect so necessary for mature moral growth of employees. When codes focus on the negative, they risk missing the big ethical issues. In other words, codes listing prohibited behaviors can "strain out a gnat but swallow a camel" because manuals of dos and don'ts fail to appreciate that not all values are equal. Some are more important than others.

Within government, codes of ethics are in force at the national and state levels. In 1978, the U.S. Congress passed an Ethics in Government Act. The purpose of the legislation was to preserve and promote the accountability and integrity of public officials. It established the Office of Government Ethics, which deals primarily with conflicts of interest at the federal level. Furthermore, several federal statutes impose restrictions on the activities of former federal employees and prohibit current federal employees from participating in matters in which they have a financial interest. One provision permanently bars a former federal employee from representing anyone other than the United States before the government in connection with any matter involving a specific party or parties if he or she participated personally and substantially in that same matter as a government employee. Also, a former employee is barred for two years from representing anyone with respect to any matter pending under his or her official responsibility within one year prior to termination of the employee's service in the area in question (U.S. General Accounting Office [GAO], 1987). Also, federal employees are prohibited from leaving government employment and going to work for contractors with whom they worked closely in their former position.

There is great difficulty in prosecuting conflict-of-interest cases as felonies, however, even though it is required in most conflict of interest statutes. Because juries rarely return felony convictions on most conflict-of-interest cases, prosecutors in both the Public Integrity Section and the Office of the U.S. Attorney for the District of Columbia are reluctant to accept such cases for prosecution. This reluctance discourages inspector generals in federal agencies from investigating allegations and referring them for prosecution to the Justice Department (U.S. GAO, 1987).

Most state governments have adopted codes of ethics for public officials and employees. The provisions of the codes usually prohibit using one's official position or office for personal gain, offering or receiving gifts, soliciting or receiving money for advice or assistance, and using or disclosing confidential information for private financial gain. They stipulate conditions for financial disclosure statements, service on regulatory boards and commissions regulating business with which a person is associated, representation of clients or constituents before state agencies, entering into contracts with state agencies, promises of future employment or favors for members of governmental regulatory agencies, notice of lobbying by former officials or employees before bodies of which such persons were members or employees, and filing of complaints by citizens.

SUMMARY

It is important that each individual feel personally ethically responsible. It is insufficient to blame someone else or some other department for one's own unethical behavior. It is not unusual for people to try to blame "them" somewhere else in the organization for breaches of ethics. But accountability requires a sense of personal responsibility.

How an individual treats others, including customers, peers, subordinates, supervisors, and competitors is affected by the way the individual is treated within the organization. There is no position in the organization that affords a moral holiday. At best, ethical standards are just plain, good common sense. It is tempting to yield to expediency when confronted with a problem, leaving the ethical struggle to someone else. But each time an ethical dilemma is presented, coworkers, superiors, and clients are watching and will note the example provided. Taking ethics into consideration can be burdensome in the short run. But in the long run, it pays off. Dealing honestly with fellow workers and clients creates a feeling of trust that eventually builds stronger relationships between people, regardless of the industry.

The purpose of ethical inquiry is to create a framework of general principles of right and wrong, what one ought to do, and what one's duties are. The ethical domain for managers focuses on the seam between morality and individual or institutional self-interest. Ethical analysis involves assessing issues and paying attention to the effects of potential decisions on the lives of those who will be affected. Ethical decision making is clearly relevant to the very fabric of administration and governance.

A focus on ethics provides an internal traffic cop to guide individual and organizational actions in a consistent manner. The question Is this the right thing to do? will guide ethical analysis, for there is no right way to do a wrong thing. Being able to answer this question guides the traffic of decisions. If you do not know where you are going, you cannot know when you get there. If you do not know what is important to you, you have no guide for making ethical decisions.

An ethical audit is a useful way of evaluating the corporate context in which one works, and from which one receives not only assignments and responsibilities but expectations and a sense of self-worth. Here are the questions to ask:

Is this the person I want to be?
Who are the heroes where I work? What are their virtues? Any notable vices?

The attributes that the heroes are known and recognized for are those which the organization values highly. The vices are those which are openly tolerated. Then, ask yourself, Do I admire the heroes? Do I want to be like them?

In the final analysis, ethical responsibility is everyone's individual responsibility. To wait for "them" elsewhere in the organization to engage in more ethical practices is to wait forever. To have an ethical organization requires three things: having a critical mass of ethically responsible individuals, promoting norms that encourage ethical behavior, and having leaders of the organization who behave ethically and serve as ethical role models for others to emulate. Since it is very difficult to control others' unethical behavior, it behooves all individuals to focus on that which they can control: their own ethical behavior.

2

Decision Making

Moral deliberation, like all kinds of deliberation, is a sort of calculus, a method of reckoning, of working out . . . which course of action is supported by the best moral reasons. . . . The procedure is very much like weighing. One can only explain the weighing machine and check the weights: the weighing itself has still to be done on each particular occasion.

—Kurt Baier

It is the responsibility of the decision maker to inject ethical considerations into the decision calculus. In the words of noted economist Herbert Simon, reason is instrumental: it cannot tell us where to go; at best it can only tell us how to get there. "It is a gun for hire that can be employed in the service of whatever goals we have, good or bad" (Simon, 1983, pp. 7–8). This chapter explores decision making to show how ethical calculations can be built into problem solving. It closes with a definition of ethical decision making and a case study.

THE DECISION CALCULUS

Policy statements, codes of ethics, and laws forbidding corrupt practices attempt to prevent breaches of ethics. But these cannot replace ethical decision making; they can only supplement what is within the individual, which is his or her own set of principles applied to each decision made. Every time a decision is reached about an administrative problem, it is resolved on the basis of assumptions that lie at the heart of a philosophy of personal and social living.

Effective decision makers rely upon a fundamental set of moral values to operate intelligently and consistently. Moral values shape the way problems are identified, defined, and solved. For example, managers ask themselves a number of questions as they solve problems: Am I addressing the right problem? Who will be harmed by this decision? What is the right thing to do? Will I regret this decision later? Will long-term gain outweigh short-term losses? Queries such as these raise issues relating to the ten core values: caring, honesty, accountability, promise keeping, pursuit of excellence, loyalty, fairness, integrity, respect for others, and responsible citizenship. These values belong in the decision because they reflect the decision's ethical component.

There are multiple ethical perspectives to most problems. Each perspective is framed by how the problem is defined and the priorities of the decision maker. In a group decision, a clash of values is disruptive when conflicting parties fail to acknowledge each other's differing priorities and instead assume that the other is not only mistaken but misguided. Inevitably, decision makers will conflict with one another because they differ over which values are most important to maximize. They are disagreeing more over what values are most moral rather than over what is immoral. While some honor obedience to time-honored routines, others believe it is more important to keep promises that have been made or to avoid hurting others. While some believe that loyalty to the company always comes first, others rank integrity higher. Each perspective stresses a different aspect of morality.

Understanding how and why people rank values differently is often the first of several important steps for arriving at an ethical decision. However, choices are rarely made directly between values. Most often they are made between options that differ in the extent to which they embody particular values or in the emphasis some values receive in one alternative compared to the emphasis they receive in another. To some degree, ethical values are fungible. While loyalty and fairness are both highly valued, loyalty may be substituted for fairness in a particular situation. Ethical choices result from choosing not between good and evil, but between competing "goods." This means selecting a good for the company versus a good for oneself, a good for a superior versus a good for a peer, or a good for the company versus a good for one's personal career.

Values penetrate all aspects of people's lives, including selection of their careers. For example, sources of job satisfaction are influenced by cultural and ideological values. Simcha Ronen (1978) found that workers from a kibbutz industry, where all workers are paid the same, report a higher level of importance attached to self-actualization values and intrinsic job rewards than do workers employed in the private sector. Employees in the private sector, where merit-based pay scales are used, report a higher level of importance attached to owning personal property. They derive job satisfaction from the extrinsic rewards of a higher salary and more status. In both groups, intrinsic values were found to be directly related to job satisfaction, but because their values differed, the rewards necessary to achieve job satisfaction differed.

THE CONTEXT OF DECISIONS

To understand ethical decision making in organizations requires an appreciation of the contingencies that surround each decision. Figure 2.1 shows how decision makers are inextricably intertwined with their environment. Their decisions are couched within the context of the situation. The decision maker is in the middle, affected by stimuli from the environment. The "right" decision is influenced by the salience of the information and pressures coming from all sides.

Many managers are subjected to a great amount of pressure to compromise their personal values in order to achieve company goals (Trevino, 1986). This is because they must balance competing demands from superiors, peers, and subordinates while simultaneously pursuing organizational goals. These circumstances are "ethical moderators" because they complicate and temper the quality of ethical decision making. The constellation of influential people combined with the demand for responsibility and accountability moderates the quality of ethical analysis and encourages expediency. This is why a person may make a work-related decision that is quite different from a decision made in one's living room unaffected by job concerns. The more complex the situation, the more variables there are to include in the decision calculus in the form of stakeholders, opportunity costs, and personal factors.

Figure 2.1
The Context of Decisions

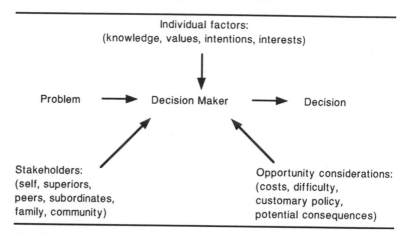

Individual factors:
(knowledge, values, intentions, interests)

Problem   ⟶   Decision Maker   ⟶   Decision

Stakeholders:
(self, superiors,
peers, subordinates,
family, community)

Opportunity considerations:
(costs, difficulty,
customary policy,
potential consequences)

THEORETICAL FRAMEWORK FOR RATIONAL DECISION MAKING

In the Western world, we applaud rationality. A rational decision is one that occurs in ordered steps and maximizes a value, whether it is honesty, efficiency, reliability, controllability, marketability, or any of many other values. Adherence to any value involves promoting one alternative over another. There are six steps to achieving a rational decision. The journey is as important as the final decision, because each step provides an opportunity to reconsider the values that are being maximized and minimized.

1. Define the problem.

   This involves isolating the key factors in question and diagnosing the situation to define the basic problem and to identify the limits of the situation. This first step is critical because it prevents solving the wrong problem.
2. Identify the goal to be achieved.

   If you do not know where you are going, you will never know when you get there. For this reason, it is essential that a goal is clearly declared.
3. List all possible solutions to the problem.

   All alternatives that will address the problem and achieve the goal are placed under consideration.
4. Evaluate each alternative to determine which one best meets the requirements of the situation.

Table 2.1
Outline for Solving Complex Problems

I. Define the problem.

II. Identify the goal to be achieved.

III. Specify all dimensions of the problem.

IV. List all possible solutions to each dimension.

V. Evaluate alternative solutions to each dimension regarding the likelihood of each to maximize the important values at stake.

VI. Eliminate alternatives which are too costly, not feasible, or maximize the wrong values when combined with solutions to other dimensions.

VII. Rank the alternatives to each dimension according to which are most likely to maximize the most important values.

VIII. Select the alternative to each dimension that is most likely to work in the context of the problem while maximizing the important values at stake.

IX. Combine the top ranking alternatives for each dimension of the problem in order to develop a solution to the problem as a whole.

X. Make a commitment to the choice and implement it.

This step requires a thorough analysis of each alternative. The analysis involves measuring the benefits, costs, and risks of each, as well as identifying the likely intended and unintended consequences of each. This step provides information about the utility of each alternative in terms of the efficiency with which it maximizes desired values and still achieves the goal.

5. Identify the one course of action that is most likely to produce the desired consequences within the constraints of the situation.

This step requires selecting the alternative that maximizes the most important values and holds the most promise of achieving the goal, while solving the problem as effectively as possible.

6. Make a commitment to the choice and implement it.
   This step requires converting the decision into action.

As time-consuming as these six steps are for solving simple one-dimensional problems, they become far more complex when the problem involves multiple dimensions—as most problems do. Each dimension becomes a problem in itself. The outline in Table 2.1 depicts how multiple dimensions of a problem are teased apart, analyzed, then combined in a ranked fashion. It goes without saying that the task of identifying all dimensions of the problem and specifying the values to be maximized is complicated.

A systematic method for identifying and ranking alternatives is the bottom-up approach. It is appropriate for situations in which the decision maker has a clear grasp of both the problem and the alternatives for solving it. In this case the primary objective of a decision analysis is to clarify the differences between the alternatives so that an informed, logical, and ethical decision can be made. Under these conditions the bottom-up, or alternative-driven, approach to value structuring has the appeal of providing a focused, efficient analysis. Once the different degree to which each alternative maximizes the important values is known, the decision maker ranks the alternatives hierarchically. This hierarchical structuring is accomplished by combining like items into categories, such as cost and quality. For example, objectives may be decreasing costs, increasing quality, and promoting a positive corporate image. Each alternative is then categorized into subparts such as start-up and ongoing costs, quality control criteria, and public relations attributes. After this process, some attributes can be dropped because it is apparent that they are redundant or that they insufficiently discriminate between alternatives. Elements can be combined or repositioned to reflect further thinking of the problem as the analysis proceeds (Buede, 1986).

RATIONAL DECISION MAKING IN REAL LIFE

The fallacy of ideal models of rational decision making is the assumption upon which they are based. They assume that tastes are absolute, relevant to the issues, consistent, and precise, when in fact none of these conditions are guaranteed (Elster, 1986). Furthermore, theoretical models assume that decision makers will take the time and energy to thoroughly investigate all dimensions of the problem. The inevitable truth is that humans fall short of perfect rationality, for it is impossible to know everything there is to know about all situations and alternatives. Moreover, personal biases and sensitivities block objective review of all aspects. Herbert Simon, who was awarded the Nobel Prize for his work on what he called "bounded rationality," says the evidence is overwhelming that the theoretical model of rational decision making does not reflect actual decision making processes. In fact, he believes the theory of decision making based solely on individual utility scales and preference ordering, without regard to the context of the decision, is as useful as a one-bladed scissors (Simon, 1987).

Amos Tversky and Daniel Kahneman (1986) argue that the most basic rules of the normative rational model are violated routinely by decision makers. They argue that the framing of decisions depends on the language of presentation, on the context of choice, and on the nature of the display, so that the treatment of the decision making process is necessarily informal and incomplete. For example, there is a significant difference in how price is framed. It is easier for a consumer to forego a discount than to accept a surcharge, because the same price difference is valued as a gain in the former case and as a loss in the latter. The credit card industry makes use of this irony by insisting that any price difference between cash and card purchases should be labeled a cash discount rather than a credit surcharge. People prefer the cup half full over the cup half empty.

Only when decision makers know the stakes are great do they invest time in more thorough analyses. Experiments show that as the benefit of making a correct decision increases, problem solvers take more time to reach a solution and are more confident in their answers (Christensen-Szalanski, 1978). A problem solver's confidence in the accuracy of his or her decision appears to be related to the fact that more important problems make potentially more accurate, complex, and costly strategies worth using.

People act rationally only if the expected outcome of their actions affords them a utility at least as great as that from any other action possible for them in the situation. The truth is that continuous or repeated choices, when they are easily visible and there are no costs in switching, allow easy, continuous adjustment to what others are doing. Thus, incremental decision making is preferred more often than the pure model of rational decision making. Successive approximations to an optimal solution are made, in contrast to ideal rationality in which a comprehensive analysis of the problem is performed and the one optimal alternative is selected once and for all.

Work decisions often fail to meet the requirements of rational decision making. Executives follow each other's lead rather than independently analyze each new problem. They acquire information through hearsay. Since beliefs and values are contagious from one person to another, most beliefs gain their credibility not from direct experience and rational analysis, but from their acceptance by credible sources in society (Simon, 1983).

Humans are intuitive statisticians and experts in efficiency when it comes to making decisions. They consider the potential payoffs and costs of engaging in various acts, but they do so pragmatically. Instead of using the ideal rational model to guide their analyses, they use approximations to the rational model. This is why people may "rationally" select a strategy for decision making that, from an outsider's point of view, appears to be capricious.

When a decision must be made hurriedly, less information is sought in the problem-solving process than if the decision maker has sufficient time to analyze the problem thoroughly. Howard Rothstein (1986) reports that time-pressured individuals tend to be more erratic than those who are not hurried. He explains that time pressure has a significant effect on human judgment, because when the time frame is too limited, some pieces of the problem are only partially evaluated.

When presented the choice, people will rely on an easy-to-understand decision rule rather than reevaluate a situation from the beginning and look for nuances not immediately noticeable (Arrow and Raynaud, 1986). John Payne, Myron Braunstein, and John Carroll (1978) found that an increased use of heuristic strategies (rules of thumb) accompany an increasing number of alternatives. Heuristics are a convenient and quick means for reducing the number of alternatives that must be evaluated.

Even purely individual decisions involve costs. Because of this, people typically routinize many everyday choices. Routines allow people to adopt a rule that dictates the solution to many questions. This reduces the costs of decision making since it requires conscious effort only when an existing rule is to be broken or modified. Most people gladly exchange complete information in favor of simple rules of thumb that help to assess probabilities.

When heuristics are triggered, people let themselves ignore information that may be far more important but less interesting or understandable. People make mistakes even when they know what they value. They will strongly prefer a price of $99 to $101, but they will say the difference between $76 and $78 is negligible. In fact, the value of $2 is the same, regardless of what two amounts it falls between.

Even though common sense tells us that people do not behave in an ideally rational manner, we cannot understand a person's behavior unless we can interpret it either as rational or as an understandable deviation from rational behavior, such as an understandable mistake, an understandable emotional reaction, or an understandable but unusual response. Irrationality is excused as an inevitable by-product of the complexity that confronts us.

Communication and discussion rest on the tacit premise that each person believes in the rationality of the others. Otherwise there would be no point to the exchange. The realistic value of a clear normative concept of rational behavior lies in the fact that it provides a guide for explaining why people deviate from this concept of rationality. In fact, the theory of rationality provides its own heuristic.

BOUNDED RATIONALITY

Researchers aware of the breach between theory and practicality have developed models that fill in where formal models of rationality are unrealistic. These models acknowledge the extent to which individuals and groups simplify a decision problem because of the difficulties of anticipating or considering all alternatives and all information. These more practical models introduce simple search and decision rules, working backward, incrementalism, uncertainty avoidance, and reliance on standard operating procedures. "Since the organism, like those of the real world, has neither the senses nor the wits to discover an 'optimal' path—even assuming the concept of optimal to be clearly defined—we are concerned only with finding a choice mechanism that will lead it to pursue a 'satisficing' path, a path that will permit satisfaction at some specified level of all of its needs" (Simon, 1957, pp. 270–71).

Bounded rationality is a term used to explain rational decision making applied to real-world situations. It occurs when a decision maker is subjected to information overload such that the information demands of the decision environment exceed one's information-processing capacity (Taylor, 1975). Limited ability causes the decision maker to formulate the problem in a simplistic manner. For example, one of the least demanding techniques for making decisions on multidimensional problems is for the decision maker to specify preference constraints and to satisfice by attempting to find a decision alternative that just meets, but not necessarily surpasses, the constraints. Charles Lindblom (1959) describes successive limited comparisons. It is a decision-making process that more nearly reflects decision making in real life.

1. Selection of goals and needed actions are not distinct, but closely intertwined.
2. Since means and ends are not distinct, means-end analysis is limited.
3. The test of a good decision is that analysts find themselves directly agreeing on a policy without their agreeing that it is the most appropriate means to an agreed objective.
4. Analysis is limited and important possible outcomes are neglected.
5. Important alternatives are neglected.
6. Important values are neglected.

Successive comparisons of alternatives involving only incremental changes from that which is already in place result in selection of the least noxious alternative. In its purest sense rationality requires a choice among all possible alternatives, but in actuality only a very few of them ever come to mind.

Since decision making is a dynamic process, it cannot be understood outside the context in which it occurs. It is affected by considerations about uncertainty, risk, people, materials, machines, resources, and any other issues present, or perceived to be present, at the time the decision is to be made. Ordinary models of rationality are inadequate to describe decision making in complex organizations, for such models fail to incorporate the context in which the decision is made. Instead, *contextual rationality* is a term that describes decision making in the real world. The term emphasizes the extent to which the generation and selection of alternatives is embedded in a complex of other claims on the attention of those making the decision.

ETHICAL SATISFICING

Human beings satisfice because they have not the wits to maximize (Simon, 1976). This is true in terms of decisions heavily laden with ethical components as well as decisions involving few ethical considerations, such as what make of car to buy. This is why decision makers ethically satisfice, just as they rationally satisfice. They come to the best decision they can given the constraints of the situation.

Complex ethical decisions have four characteristics:

a. Two or more values are affected by the decision.
b. A comparison between the values is inevitable, such that a greater return to one can be obtained only at a loss to the other.
c. Uncertainty prevails, meaning that not everything is known about the situation and anticipated consequences cannot be predicted with certainty.
d. The power to make the decision is dispersed over a multitude of individual actors and/or organizational units.

Executives are often disgruntled when they learn that decisions made farther down the chain of command fail to maximize the values they consider most important. One reason less-than-best decisions occur is that those making the decisions are concerned not so much with the optimality of the decision as with its acceptability to their boss, peers, or subordinates. The advantage of many suboptimal decisions is that they have the least uncertainty and generate the least amount of interpersonal friction (Johnson, 1974). The disadvantage is that they represent the lowest common denominator of all the stakeholders' preferences. The decision avoids conflict but also fails to maximize any important value other than an innocuous compromise.

The decisions and behavior of upper-level managers have a strong influence on subordinate performance. Actions speak louder than words. Terry Cooper (1986) argues that an organization's members learn to read its values and ethical standards through the conduct of its upper echelons and through the way it allocates resources. The entire process is fragile, with one instance of an employee experiencing retribution from a resentful boss for engaging in courageous ethical conduct obliterating ten instances of rewards. This drives the real moral heroes into whistle-blowing outside the organization.

Fundamental values, principles, and goals must be clarified and unambiguously communicated before those with decision-making responsibilities understand the values to maximize. Because of the proclivity for people to "satisfice," they will seek rules of thumb regarding which values are most important. In an ideal world a decision maker will determine the fundamental values to be fostered by a decision and then weigh the probable impact of each alternative. In reality, the decision maker will analyze the most obvious values involved and determine which of several alternatives will maximize the value that is understood to be most important. A full consideration of all dimensions of the problem will not occur. This is why the most important values must be clearly communicated, so at least these will be maximized.

Studies that investigate ethical decision making conclude that a perceived sense of responsibility for behaving ethically significantly increases the quality of ethical decision making. Research on group decision making also shows that accountability enhances the likelihood of ethical decision making. Effective problem solving and friendly cooperation are especially likely to accrue to negotiators who have a deep concern about their own side's welfare and yet who also have, or desire to establish, a positive relationship with each other. Orly Ben-Yoav and Dean Pruitt (1984) explain this. They studied expectation of cooperative future interaction and concluded that expectations build accountability into the decision-making process. When there was no expectation of cooperative future interaction, negotiators were contentious and adversarial. But when the expectation for cooperative future interaction was present, negotiators were more conciliatory and generated an amicable compromise. These results suggest that decision-making behavior is a function of both a concern for personal goals and a concern for the relationship with the other party.

Because most work-related decisions that involve significant moral components are decided by a group rather than an individual, Mary Nichols and Victoria Day (1982) compared decision-making styles in groups. They compared an interacting group to a nominal group and found the level of moral judgment to be higher in the interacting group. The data suggested that the higher-scoring individuals shifted their positions less and presumably influenced group decisions more, persuading those who relied on lower levels of moral judgment to rise to the occasion and espouse a more ethical solution.

Another study focused on the effect of accountability on decision-making effort. Kenneth Price (1987) found that individuals who were held responsible for the quality of the decision making task, either individually or as a group, exerted more effort than those who participated anonymously and knew they would not be held accountable.

Elizabeth Weldon and Gina Gargano (1985) studied decision making in groups in which responsibility for the quality of complex judgments was shared. They found that those who believed that responsibility for the task was shared produced fewer evaluations and used less complex decision-making strategies than individual evaluators. These findings, as well as Price's (1987), indicate that decision makers tend to loaf when responsibility for information processing is shared.

Having to justify one's decisions also leads to higher consistency. Roger Hagafors and Berndt Brehmer (1983) found that having to justify one's judgments to others leads to higher consistency in the logic used to explain the judgment, especially when there is a high degree of uncertainty in the decision problem.

APPLYING ETHICAL ANALYSIS TO DECISION MAKING

Openness and ethics go together. Actions that are unethical will often not withstand scrutiny. Openness in arriving at decisions reflects the same logic. It gives those with an interest in a particular decision the chance to make their views known and opens to argument the basis on which the decision is finally made. Disclosure is not a panacea for improving the quality of ethical decisions, but the willingness to operate an open system is the foundation for promoting ethics in everyday decisions (Cadbury, 1987).

Ethical decision making, like economics, deals with the decision-making concepts of preferences, utilities, costs, benefits, goals, and objectives. The decision maker's challenge is to operationalize and quantify moral values and liken the process to nonmoral decision making. Cost/benefit analysis is the notion that one can measure costs and benefits by reducing everything to a dollar value. This is its ease but also its drawback. Even its most enthusiastic partisans admit that cost/benefit analysis needs to be supplemented by consideration of additional values, such as judgments about equity. Social life is rarely captured in static situations where the costs and benefits of an alternative are unrelated to any other. To maximize one value is to minimize another.

Plato conceived of the ultimate Good as a concept encompassing a hierarchy of values (Leys, 1968). Plato never indicated that the final Good can be defined, but the vague notion of an ultimate, ordering principle justified all of his efforts to resolve particular conflicts. On a scale of values, particular objectives comprise the lowest level of a Platonic value scale, and above that level appear more abstract criteria for choosing among objectives. A Platonic value scale in terms of the ten core values applied to the world of work might look something like this:

1. The idea of the Good
2. Organizational standards
    a. Responsible citizenship
    b. Pursuit of excellence
    c. Accountability
3. Interpersonal standards
    a. Fairness
    b. Promise keeping
    c. Loyalty
    d. Caring for others
    e. Respect for others
4. Personal standards
    a. Honesty
    b. Integrity

The construction of an inflexible value scale is an absurdity, since such a scale would have to include values in a rigid ordering and yet be applicable to all situations. In a given circumstance, however, and for a limited period of time, there is no absurdity in supposing that a rank ordering of values can be established by thoughtful deliberation. What is helpful about a value scale is that it forces people to think about everything that they value instead of focusing on one or two values to the exclusion of others. Even though value scales can be useful, the fact remains that during the actual decision-making task, people are cognitively capable of seriously evaluating only two or three values at a time.

Facet Analysis

Facet analysis is a methodology in which the facets of a problem are identified and agreed upon by decision makers, based on their common definition of the problem (Shapira and Zevulun, 1979). Once all facets are identified, then each alternative is evaluated according to its capacity to respond to the facets of the problem and still achieve the goal.

Uncovering the ethical nuances of a problem can be made easier by using the concept of facets. Ethical considerations are one facet of a decision problem, just as costs and quality control are facets. A problem can be approached by identifying its many facets.

Dialectical Inquiry

Dialectical inquiry is an approach to decision making that involves examining a decision completely and logically from two different and opposing points of view (Schwenk, 1984). First, a prevailing or recommended plan is identified, along with the data that were used to derive it. Then an attempt is made to identify the assumptions underlying the plan. A counterplan is developed that is feasible, politically viable, and generally credible but which rests on assumptions opposite to those that support the plan. Next a structured debate is conducted in which those responsible for making the decision hear arguments in support of both the plan and the counterplan. This debate, in contrast to a traditional management briefing, consists of a forceful presentation of two opposing plans, each of which rests on different interpretations of the same information.

The dialectical-inquiry approach is superior to an expert approach because with the latter, recommendations contain hidden assumptions that frequently are not communicated to management. It is superior to devil's advocacy because it explores assumptions on both sides of the question, not just those that oppose the plan. Dialectical inquiry introduces a healthy dose of conflict into the calculus. Conflict serves to provide a deeper analysis of assumptions, interpretations, possible options, and evaluations of alternatives. The result is that examination of the problem with its varied facets and possible solutions is improved (Rose, Menasco, and Curry, 1982).

DEFINITION OF ETHICAL DECISION MAKING

Ethical decision making is the process of identifying a problem, generating alternatives, and choosing among them so that the alternatives selected maximize the most important ethical values while also achieving the intended goal. Implicit within this definition is the acknowledgment that not all values can be maximized simultaneously. Some must be compromised in order for others to be maximized. This compromise is ethical satisficing, that is, pursuing a decision path that will permit satisfaction at some specified level of ethical need. The strategic ethical response is simply the best response under the circumstances. To evaluate the best response, a manager must take into account not just immediate profitability but the company's reputation, its long-term survival, the happiness and well-being of those affected, and the integrity of the pursuit itself.

Decisions that combine ethical and work-related judgments are challenging. The first step is to determine as precisely as possible what one's personal rules of conduct are. The second step is to decide who else will be affected by the decision and how much weight to assign to their interests. It is easier to judge the morality of decisions if one ignores the context in which the decision had to be made. The evaluation is not worthwhile, however, unless it takes the context into consideration. If what would be considered corruption in the company's home territory is an accepted business practice elsewhere, how are local managers expected to act? The following case shows the dilemma one man faced when he was assigned to work in a culture different from that to which he was accustomed and different from what the organization's standard operating procedures prescribed.

Case: Ethical Decision Making amidst Contrasting Cultural Norms

Military officers assigned as advisors to foreign armies have no "command authority" over the units to which they are assigned. Their ability to effect positive changes is contingent on their personal rapport with their host country counterpart. In the early 1970s, John Donohue was assigned as an advisor to a Korean military police unit.

Public ethics in Korea are (or at least were at that time) very different from those of the United States. Public servants were paid very low wages. In many cases, a midlevel bureaucrat would earn less than a day laborer. It was expected that a Korean official would make most of his income from tips or gifts provided by individuals who needed his assistance.

Officials of the United States, including military advisors, received American-made goods through special commissaries that did not have to pay the very high Korean import taxes (often over 200 percent), and so paid much less than Koreans had to pay for similar items in the local markets. U.S. personnel were prohibited by treaty from selling or giving duty-free goods to any Korean.

One day, Donohue's interpreter reminded him that the lunar New Year was coming up. This is a big holiday in Asian countries, a time when gift giving is traditional. His predecessors, he was informed, had always given each Korean officer a bottle of a very expensive Scotch whisky as a New Year's present. When he reminded his interpreter that this was illegal, the interpreter admitted that it was, but pointed out that the Koreans always gave the advisors a very nice gift on the Fourth of July, so they would be angry if the advisors did not reciprocate. Besides, the interpreter added, the advisors could easily forge documents to indicate that the liquor was consumed at an official function held at a U.S. facility. That way Donohue could use government funds to pay for the gifts and, also, he would not have to use any of his limited liquor ration to secure the gifts.

Ethical Issues

He was caught in a dilemma. He did not want to compromise his excellent relationship with his counterparts, because then he would not be able to do his job. On the other hand, he did not want to violate the law on duty-free goods. Even less did he want to falsify records to cover the diversion of liquor. Finally, since his predecessors had accepted substantial gifts for doing their job, his conscience told him that he should officially report the whole matter as a violation of the army's conflict-of-interest regulations.

The competing values were *pursuit of excellence* (getting the job done) and *loyalty* (to his fellow officers and organization) versus *honesty, promise keeping* (obeying his oath to uphold laws and regulations), *accountability* (reporting violations), and *integrity*.

Alternatives

No matter what he did, someone was going to be angry. As a result, he was angry over being placed in that position. His initial reaction was to say "to hell with it," and go along with the established practice. However, if he did so, then any of the Koreans who knew that he had violated the law, and there would be many, might use that information as leverage to make him lean toward their interpretation of policies when there was a conflict between what they wanted and what Donohue's American superiors wanted.

Resolution

In the end, Donohue decided that he would not report the conflict-of-interest violations by his predecessors, because it was unlikely that any disciplinary or criminal action would be taken. The violators were already back in the United States, and hard evidence to back up a charge would be difficult to produce. If he filed an official complaint, there would be a lot of hard feelings, and little good would be accomplished.

On the other hand, he realized that much could be done, unofficially, to eliminate the problem in the future. He went to his boss to explain the situation. He explained that he was not willing to covertly divert liquor to be used as gifts, nor was he willing to falsify the records to cover it up. Donohue's superior was not happy about his having raised the issue. After debating the merits of giving gifts to the Koreans, Donohue and his boss worked out the following compromise: Donohue would give the gifts using his own money to buy the liquor; he would officially document the gifts using a memorandum for record, which he would forward to his boss. The boss would forward the memorandum to headquarters with a recommendation that some adjustment to the regulations be made to cover the provision of gifts. Donohue also asked his interpreters to explain to his Korean counterparts that he would not accept any gifts.

Donohue could live with the compromise. His superior was satisfied because Donohue's relationship with his counterparts was not damaged and the boss was off the hook as far as sanctioning the gifts. Donohue's superior passed the buck to his boss. Headquarters, however, refused to change the regulations to sanction the gifts.

Donohue's counterparts were puzzled, but not angry, at his refusal to accept gifts. For occasions when they had traditionally sent gifts, they would send Donohue a letter of appreciation instead. He continued to document the purchases of liquor for gifts and pay for it himself for the rest of his tour. The gifts were always made a matter of public record, but no one ever censured him for violating the regulations on disposition of duty-free goods (Donohue, 1988).

Identifying the ethical issues in this decision-making process involves outlining the overall decision-making process and the context within which it occurred. Donohue's goal was to maintain rapport with his counterparts and yet not violate army regulations. He wanted to maintain his integrity by not lying about gift giving and yet he realized that gift giving was an expected custom. Cultural differences built ethical moderators into the decision calculus.

Six of the ten values in CHAPELFIRZ are called into play in this dilemma: honesty, accountability, promise keeping, pursuit of excellence, loyalty, and integrity. Donohue chose to maximize pursuit of excellence when he decided it was critical to maintain a positive rapport with his Korean counterparts in order to fulfill his duty assignment. He maximized loyalty by deciding not to report his predecessors for gift giving. He maximized honesty by carefully documenting his violation of the regulation prohibiting gift giving and receiving. He maximized integrity by remaining true to his personal value by avoiding a conflict of interest. He maximized accountability by publicly documenting his activities and being open and public about his decision. In order to maximize these values, his compromise minimized the values of promise keeping by violating his oath to uphold all regulations, even those prohibiting giving and receiving gifts.

It is up to you to determine if this compromise was the best that could be accomplished given these circumstances. In summary, and very simply, the operational choices that Donohue made in the face of the issues presented in this situation allowed him to sleep well at night, a simple test not without its merits as a device for reviewing one's ethical "inventory." Remember, the decisions, however painful, that leave one feeling like a whole person are usually best.

SUMMARY

Notwithstanding the complexity of rational decision making, loading a problem with ethical considerations makes it even more challenging. Just as the model for rational decision making prescribes, arriving at an ethical decision requires the decision maker to bring ethical values into the decision calculus, along with all other components of the problem to be solved. Because a thorough analysis of all possible alternative solutions to the problem is beyond the capacity of the human mind, especially when beset by a conglomeration of other pressures on the job, "satisficing" occurs with ethical decision making just as it does with simpler decisions that have no ethical component. The more facets there are to consider, the more complex it becomes.

Realistic decision making maximizes the most important values while acknowledging that trade-offs are inevitable. Lest a paralysis of analysis were to set in, it is incumbent on the decision maker to determine which values are most important, see that they are maximized without unduly minimizing other positive values, and move forward with the decision. The courage to act on one's decisions is as much a part of the decision-making process as is the analytic step of assessing alternatives.

Part II

Applying Ethical Decision Making

3

Interpersonal Relationships

Ethics should not be perceived as a moral guideline but as a cooperative, basic working social principle.

—Ivan Hill

The work of the manager involves planning, organizing, staffing, directing, coordinating, reporting, and budgeting. All of these managerial functions require interacting with other people in order for them to be performed well. Interactions are necessary across hierarchical ranks and departmental lines. They involve relations with peers, with superiors, and with subordinates. The standards practiced by management during these interactions become the touchstone of an organization's culture.

Employees' moral judgments reflect the norms of the organization. Company guidelines, traditions, and expectations creep into their own normative judgments, such that ambience and ethics often become one. A company that is good to be with inspires goodness, too. But being a company that is good to be with and one that inspires goodness is easier said than done. H. R. Smith and Archie Carroll (1984) argue that the deck is stacked against ethical decision making in organizations. As a result of superiors using hierarchical leverage to take the ethical dimension of decision making away from subordinates, the stage is set for a "they-made-me-do-it" defense by lower-level employees when violations of ethical norms come to light. There is also the "I-made-them-do-it" situation in which those lower in the hierarchy prefer to nest in the technical aspects of their work and delegate tough choices upward.

Employees who look to their superiors for ethical guidance often complain that pressure for improper conduct comes from above. Pressure comes to support incorrect viewpoints, to purposefully underestimate costs in a bid, to falsify lists of achievements, to overlook wrongful acts by superiors, or to conduct business with friends of superiors (Rein, 1980). These ethical trespasses emphasize the importance of including the ethical dimension in individual as well as group decisions. At least some, if not all, of the values in CHAPELFIRZ enter into most of these decisions, and they often do so in a "messy" fashion. "Messy" problems are those that are accompanied by ambiguity, uncertainty, and no explicitly happy ending for all stakeholders. Instead, any solution to the problem results in sharply contrasting outcomes, with benefits for some and harm for others.

CONTRADICTORY NORMS

Contradictory norms often compete with one another. The combination of social and political forces creates a tension in the workplace. Workers expect equality in a capitalist marketplace that is inherently unequal. Democracy and the free market do not function in a simple, cooperative arrangement. It is difficult to reconcile the values of a free market, which implies inequality, with democracy, which implies equality. The interaction of American-style democracy and American-style capitalism produces a unique business climate comprising a truncated free-market economy operating within a truncated democracy. The conflicts in this curious blend are brought to light in the various roles that employers and employees fill. While some roles require democratic priorities, others require market priorities. The oscillation between roles and subroles, accompanied by respective norms and counternorms, challenges a person's ability to make consistent ethical choices, since that which is most important differs according to the exigencies encountered by different roles.

Openness, honesty, and candor are juxtaposed against distrust of one's competition. Win-lose competition exists between personnel, and people engage in defensive routines to protect themselves. For example,

Table 3.1
Norms and Counternorms

Norms	Counternorm
Be open	Play your cards close to your vest
Be objective	Get emotionally involved
Follow the rules	Get the job done -- any way you can
Be cost efficient	Spend it or burn it
Be a team player	Look out for Number One
Take responsibility	Pass the Buck
Do it now	Never do today what you can do tomorrow

assume that a colleague, Joseph, is an on-the-way-to-the-top, stop-at-nothing sort of person who has the reputation of being ruthless in dealing with other employees. Assume Joseph sidles up to you one day, is warm and friendly for the first time since you have known him, and then asks you for a favor. You will process what he has said defensively. Anyone who knows Joseph would. Past experience and treatment say be wary. This is normal defensiveness. On the other hand, consider those who *always* process what is said to them defensively. Not being able to trust others hampers the flow of ideas that is vital to organizations as well as to interpersonal relationships. The climate within an organization either encourages or discourages defensive encounters. When interpersonal communication within a company is characterized by defensiveness, the company reflects that same degree of defensiveness.

Table 3.1 lists norms and counternorms. Instilling a sense of personal responsibility and adherence to constructive norms is challenging because adherence to the countervailing norms often represents the easier way to do things (Jansen and Von Glinow, 1985). In some situations the counternorm is more productive than the norm. The challenge is knowing when to invoke one over the other.

Objectivity is juxtaposed against emotional involvement. People are urged to be objective, as if they have no personal stake in an issue. On the other hand, the best way to motivate personnel to do a job well is to convince them that they have a personal stake in the effort. One must be responsible for one's own success in order to feel the intrinsic reward of pride in one's work and achievements. When people are responsible for their own failure, the absence of rewards is keenly felt. Research shows that when people do not control their level of performance, they exhibit only low levels of motivation (Fisher, 1978). Success is rarely meaningful unless it is brought about by one's own efforts.

Following the rules is juxtaposed against breaking the rules to get the job done. There is a tacit understanding in most companies that an organization would come to a grinding halt if everyone narrowly followed the rules to the letter. Some degree of maneuvering room has to be left open to circumvent standard procedures so that important matters can be expedited. Although maneuvering room is essential, slippage is a threat. When Jeb Magruder referred to his involvement in the Watergate scandal as a matter of "slippage" he was referring to unintentional deviations from acceptable conduct that occur because certain actions are justified in the name of some acceptable goal—such as profits or political gain. Once a goal is established, the means to achieve it can become a secondary matter, and such slippage becomes a possibility. Slippage starts as a small misrepresentation, perhaps mislabeling a product or withholding communications from employees. The next slip occurs more easily and leads to a more serious problem (Rein, 1980).

INTERPERSONAL ETHICAL DILEMMAS

Interpersonal dilemmas are best approached by first answering the two questions, Who counts? and How to measure worth? (Pastin, 1984). Who counts? refers to who the stakeholders are and, among them, whose interests have priority. The question How to measure worth? refers to calculating the utility of the values that are included in the decision calculus. Before too many dilemmas have been addressed, all ten core values will have been drawn upon. Concerns about caring, honesty, accountability, promise keeping, pursuit of excellence, loyalty, fairness, integrity, respect for others, and responsible citizenship influence decisions that affect the well-being of others. The situations explored in this chapter present examples of dilemmas met frequently on the job. The analysis accompanying each case includes an evaluation of the values involved and the impact of the situation on the stakeholders.

The cases that follow touch on various aspects of interpersonal relationships. "The Incompetent Supervisor" deals with a subordinate's quandary about how to improve the work of the person who supervised her. "Dealing with an Inept Colleague and an Ineffectual Supervisor" explores a situation that a group of teachers found themselves in when one of their colleagues was inept and the principal would not remedy the problem. "Transferring Staff against Their Will" addresses what happens when personnel are reassigned against their will. "Personal Needs versus Organizational Needs" focuses on the choice a superior must make about whether to put the best interest of the organization ahead of an employee's best interest. "Supervising Friends" targets those touchy situations in which a newly promoted supervisor must discipline a subordinate who, until recently, had been the new supervisor's personal friend. "Handling Sexual Harassment" reports the awkwardness a new employee experienced when confronted with unwanted sexual innuendoes from her new boss. "A Problem of Accountability when Firing Others" focuses on the dilemma that arose when a superior had given an alcoholic employee an opportunity to rehabilitate himself, only to find that the effort had failed. "The Problem of Promise Keeping" demonstrates the choice an employer must make when deciding how honest to be when asked for an employment reference on a former employee. "The Problem of Integrity" is a closely related case. It details the problems that occur when personal obligations threaten to compromise one's honest appraisal of a former employee.

Case: The Incompetent Supervisor

This is the case of Rebecca Smalley, a bookkeeper in a small not-for-profit human service agency. She was supervised by the business manager and was responsible for keeping the books and billing clients. Claims were being filed promptly and the revenue base was increasing until the business manager started having personal problems. Smalley knew that the business manager and his wife were on the verge of separating. When his marital problems began, he started missing deadlines, and the quality of his work deteriorated. He took numerous annual leave days, was late processing vouchers for reimbursement, and almost caused the agency to miss meeting a payroll on time. Filing of insurance claims fell behind schedule. When Smalley saw that her supervisor's personal problems were jeopardizing the good of the agency, she talked to him to let him know that even though he was the supervisor, he was jeopardizing the welfare of the agency by his inaction. He thanked her for the talk, expressed agreement with her assessment, and promised to get back on schedule. However, his work only became worse. This made Smalley, who took pride in keeping her work up-to-date, fall behind. But she was uneasy about going over the business manager's head to report his deteriorating work to the executive director. So she waited until directly confronted by the executive director to explain the problem.

Ethical Issues

Smalley felt the business manager was violating *promise keeping*. He was being neither true to his word nor trustworthy. By not performing his job duties he was causing those whose job performance was dependent on his output to fail. He violated *caring* and *respect for others* as well as disregarding the *pursuit of excellence*. On the other hand, Smalley was caught between *loyalty* to her supervisor and loyalty to the well-being of the organization. If she showed *respect for others* by not going over his head to report the situation, then she would minimize the values of *loyalty, pursuit of excellence*, and *honesty* regarding the organization.

The dilemma in this case was that Smalley took pride in doing good work, but her performance was solely dependent on her receiving work from the business manager before she could act on it. When he performed poorly, so did she, and this had a negative effect on her output and jeopardized other personnel when the payroll was late or the cash flow was too low to meet the payroll. Because of her *loyalty* to the business manager, Smalley was reluctant to go over his head and report the difficulty to the director. She cared for her supervisor and did not want to call unnecessary attention to his personal problems. But she took pride in the pursuit of excellence and in the agency's excellent performance.

Alternatives

Several alternatives were available to Smalley. She could have gone directly to the executive director and reported her supervisor's problems, but this would have violated her respect for him, her loyalty to him, and her desire not to bring his personal problems to the attention of the executive director. She could have ignored the problems altogether, but this would have violated the pursuit of excellence.

If she covered for her supervisor, she would not have been encouraging him to be accountable for his actions. By allowing his performance to influence her job performance, she would have compromised her personal commitment to the pursuit of excellence.

She could have responded indignantly to the director's inquiry, defending her supervisor and admonishing the agency for not being more caring about her supervisor's personal problems. She could have then suggested that her supervisor be given special assistance until he got his personal problems straightened out. This approach would have maximized caring, loyalty to her supervisor, and respect for her supervisor. It would have minimized any responsibility on the supervisor's part to keep his promise to do better work, it would have jeopardized fairness in terms of his being treated differently from other employees, and it would have threatened the executive director's faith in Smalley's integrity.

Or Smalley could have explained to the director about the discussions she had already had with her supervisor in which she pointed out to him how deficient his work had become. She could have reminded the director of the stress the supervisor was under and asked that provisions be made to help her department return to its normal rate of productivity. This response would have maximized caring, honesty, accountability, pursuit of excellence, loyalty, fairness, integrity, and respect for others. The only value it would have minimized to a significant degree is that of the implied promise to her supervisor not to disclose the nature of his problems to anyone else.

Resolution

In the actual case, she chose to talk with the business manager and wait to see if his work improved. When it did not, out of loyalty to her supervisor she chose to wait until the director came to her to ask about the problems. This solution minimized the pursuit of excellence from an agency standpoint but maximized loyalty to her immediate supervisor and caring and respect for him.

Winning supervisors make winning teams. If a supervisor communicates high expectations to subordinates and rewards achievements, subordinates tend to perform to expectation. On the other hand, when supervisors fail to reward productive behavior and fail to sanction poor performers, then everyone suffers—except the poor performers. The next case demonstrates this dilemma.

Case: Dealing with an Inept Colleague and an Ineffectual Supervisor

In this example a newly hired public school teacher, Jim Williams, joined the high school faculty appearing unusually insecure in his position. The experienced teachers took him under their wing and helped him as much as they could until each, one by one, gave up upon realizing that Williams's insecurities and ineptitude went far deeper than they had first assumed. He had come to the job with a previous year's experience at another school in the district, and the experienced teachers began to wonder how the principal could have brought on such a bad hire if she had done a thorough reference check. Williams was inept at teaching, record keeping, collegiality, and virtually everything else that a teacher should be able to do well. When it became obvious that the new teacher was not working out, the principal did not counsel him. Instead, she ignored the problems. When the problems did not disappear, she reacted with disgust and anger, making threats right and left. She began keeping meticulous records. She "tightened the thumbscrews" in every way possible, hoping he would quit. So as not to be accused of discrimination, she tightened up on everyone, good and bad alike. The teachers went to the principal and tried to persuade her to relieve Williams of his duties for his sake and the sake of the students. But the principal refused to do so. Finally, in order to appease the complaints from Williams's students, the other teachers volunteered to take over most of the poor teacher's duties.

Ethical Issues

Although the principal was responsible for maintaining equitable work loads, she failed to be accountable for her inaction and the effect it had on the other teachers. This case involves *accountability* for one's decisions, in that the principal had made a bad decision to hire Williams. The situation worsened when she refused to reverse her decision as Williams's problems became obvious to his colleagues and his students. The principal allowed the work to be *unfairly* distributed among Williams's colleagues, who then had to perform their own work plus his. This was a failure to *pursue excellence* on the principal's part, countered by a desire to maintain excellence on the part of the teachers who filled in where Williams failed.

Alternatives

Several alternatives were available to the teachers. They could have totally ignored the situation and told the complaining students it was not the teachers' responsibility to compensate for Williams's failings. They could have carried their demands over the principal's head to the district school superintendent and reported not only the teacher but the principal, or they could have continued to coach Williams and deny that he had any serious problems.

Resolution

The teachers chose to compensate for Williams's failing by taking on added responsibilities. That is, they chose to pursue excellence even at the expense of the time it took out of their already full day. They chose to remain loyal to the principal and not go over her head to report the problems to the district superintendent. Their solution minimized accountability on the part of the principal and maximized loyalty to her and pursuit of excellence in spite of Williams's inadequacy. To a large degree their solution perpetuated Williams's problems, because he was allowed to stay on the job even though his performance was below minimal standards. Rather, he was learning that others would take over his duties for him and he could still retain his job.

Supervisors must deal with the behaviors of individuals in a social context, not the isolated behavior of a single person. Individuals in groups look to others to learn appropriate behaviors and attitudes. Standards become institutionalized through the adoption of roles, standard operating procedures, and group norms. When any one employee flagrantly violates these standards, the others feel as if they are being treated unfairly. Group cohesion is threatened. When a supervisor tolerates violations of accepted norms, it threatens the entire group because they wonder whether new rules have come into play.

The issue of fairness comes up often for supervisors as they struggle with the best way to reassign staff. The following case demonstrates this.

Case: Transferring Staff against Their Will

Due to staffing imbalances caused by extraordinary attrition in the southern branch office of a large federal agency, Ed Rush's northern branch office was now overstaffed while the southern office was significantly understaffed. As a result, Rush had to transfer personnel from the overstaffed office to the understaffed office, which was over three hundred miles away. Other alternatives, such as allowing attrition in the overstaffed area while hiring at the understaffed area or using temporary assignments and overtime were prevented by budgetary restrictions. After an unsuccessful attempt to resolve the problem through voluntary transfers, the only option available was involuntary assignment. As defined in the union contract, the method of selection required selecting those employees with least agency seniority. After consulting with the union, the first transfers were made according to the required procedure: they were randomly selected from among those employees who had the least length of service. As a result of those selections, one of the best employees to be reassigned resigned from the agency rather than relocate. The second round of reassignments required two more transfers. It was made clear to all employees that there might need to be even more transfers in the future.

Ed Rush did not like to force transfers because of the negative effect that reassignments had on morale and productivity. But he was also frustrated because employees had been hired with the warning that they might have to relocate. He felt that those who threatened to resign if they were reassigned had been less than truthful when they accepted such a condition of employment.

Ethical Issues

The dilemma was one of *honesty*, in terms of whether job applicants had been honest when they said during the job interview that they would be willing to relocate; *fairness*, in terms of Rush's being evenhanded in selecting who would have to be reassigned; *respect for others*, in terms of understanding the different situations of each employee and the different hardships that a relocation would bring; *caring*, in terms of appreciating how the reassignment would affect the personnel; *accountability*, in that Ed Rush was responsible for seeing that the understaffed office kept running smoothly; and *pursuit of excellence*, in that Rush wanted to keep productivity up in both offices. An additional value at stake was Rush's *integrity*. He had to resist pressure from his employees and make an independent judgment as to the best way to institute the transfers. At the same time, he had to *respect* the plight of those who were already working in the understaffed office. For them to maintain the required level of productivity, they had to have more employees.

Alternatives

Unfortunately Rush had no alternatives. He was bound by the conditions of the union contract. He could not choose another method for reassigning staff. And to maintain proper service levels, the southern branch office had to be adequately staffed.

Resolution

Rush's resolution was not an easy one. Although he relied on standard procedures for reassigning staff, this was not seen as equitable by the personnel. Rather than move, some employees resigned. The resolution taken had been prescribed by a labor-management agreement in the union contract. It maximized fairness if one agrees with the rule that those with least seniority must bear the brunt of such reassignments. While it minimized caring for others and taking their individual circumstances into consideration, it maximized honesty, since it required personnel to live up to their employment agreement to accept reassignment.

Implicit in any employment contract is the mutual understanding that the employee will contribute toward the goals of the organization in exchange for inducements, such as salary, position, and status. When a person's needs and an organization's needs are mutually exclusive, ethical problems arise. The next case shows how.

Case: Personal Needs versus Organizational Needs

This is a case of promise keeping and using personnel as means to the organization's ends. The promotion system for army officers was very competitive in the mid–1970s. The two most important factors used to determine which officers would be promoted were demonstrated performance and past job assignments. In order for captains to be promoted, it was important that they demonstrated competence serving as a company commander. Captain Johnson had served for a year in Korea, without his family, and was eagerly awaiting his return to the United States in one more month. The captain was coming up for consideration for promotion to major, but he had not yet served as a company commander. His battalion commander promised Johnson that he would be assigned to command a company if he would extend his tour in Korea for another year. He accepted, over the objections of his wife and children. Before the captain had assumed his new duties, the battalion underwent an evaluation and the personnel office failed miserably. It was clear that an experienced personnel officer was needed. Since the captain had previous experience as a personnel officer, the battalion commander assigned Johnson as the personnel officer rather than as the company commander.

Ethical Issues

The dilemma for the battalion commander was this: He had already promised the captain the opportunity to be a company commander. He was caught between breaking his promise to the captain and seriously jeopardizing Johnson's chances for promotion or disregarding Johnson's career goals and making Johnson sacrifice still more by spending another year in a foreign-duty station. The battalion commander was responsible for insuring that his organization operated at peak efficiency. *Pursuit of excellence, accountability*, and *loyalty* to his superiors demanded that he use his resources optimally to insure that the battalion was combat-ready, and it was clear to him that he would not be able to do this without assigning Johnson as personnel officer. Since the battalion commander believed that accomplishing the mission took priority over all other considerations, including the welfare of the troops, he assigned Johnson to the personnel office. Captain Johnson was not happy about the arrangement but accepted it and did good work. Ultimately, the assignment caused Johnson to be denied further promotion since he had never served as a company commander.

This dilemma juxtaposes the pursuit of excellence and loyalty to the organization against *caring for others* and *promise keeping*. It was important that the battalion worked at peak efficiency. On the other hand, it was important to develop one's good staff and see that they received promotions. The battalion commander was promoting the welfare of the personnel office by putting Captain Johnson in charge of it. Although the organization would benefit from this placement, Johnson would not benefit and would have to go through personal hardships while in that position. The battalion commander had to balance his loyalty to the army with his loyalty to the personnel under him.

Alternatives

One alternative resolution was for the commander to have found someone else to fill the personnel officer slot. This would have taken time and sacrificed excellence, but maximized caring and respect for Johnson, as well as promise keeping. Another alternative was for Johnson to have accepted the assignment as personnel officer. To do this would have maximized promise keeping, loyalty to the army, pursuit of excellence, responsible citizenship, and accountability to the army. But it would have minimized loyalty to and caring for his family. A third alternative was for both the battalion commander and Captain Johnson to have compromised. They could have come to an agreement to let Johnson take the assignment as personnel officer for a specified period of time until a new officer could be trained. The time in which Johnson was to serve in this temporary position would be limited, to allow him the opportunity to move up to a company-commander position elsewhere very soon. This compromise would have ensured that the problems in the personnel office were cleaned up and would also have preserved Johnson's career mobility.

Resolution

In actuality, when Johnson agreed to stay on as personnel officer, excellence and loyalty to the organization were maximized and Johnson paid the price with his career reaching a stalemate. This decision marks loyalty to the organization higher than caring for individual officers.

The battalion commander had a tough choice to make, and Johnson's career was at stake. Ethical problems "come with the territory" of managing people. When people are harmed in some way, when their jobs are lost or their careers stymied, when reductions in force must be made, the right way to do it must be decided. And the way that serves the interest of the organization may not serve the best interests of the individual employee. The rights of the employees and those of the employer must be balanced against each other.

COUNSELING THE PROBLEM EMPLOYEE

Research indicates that supervisors vary in their perceptions of employee problems and in their responses to marginal employees. Findings show that supervisors who are unafraid to use sanctions have higher performance ratings than those who use them less often. Findings also indicate that sanctions are not used frequently or against a wide range of subordinates, but are typically concentrated on the occasional difficult employee (O'Reilly and Weitz, 1980). The problem of marginal employees is exaggerated when they are the supervisor's friends, as the next case shows.

Case: Supervising Friends

Being promoted above one's peers with the sudden responsibility to supervise former friends is tough enough. But when one of the friends becomes a problem employee, the problem is even worse. This is a case of an employee in the accounting department of a large retail store. Sheila Ranton was an employee in the accounting department along with four other employees. She had developed both a personal and a professional relationship with most of them. They were friends as well as coworkers. There was a major reorganization and the accounting department was affected. Ranton was promoted to supervisor of the department and reported to the director of administrative services. After she was promoted, several changes took place. She was now her former coworkers' supervisor rather than just being "one of them." She now had to supervise their work. She had to distance herself enough to be respected yet still maintain a personal relationship with them. Shortly after being promoted, she encountered a situation in which one of the employees was not doing her job. She was having several personal problems that were beginning to affect her work performance. She began coming in late and using the phone too much for her personal use. Deadlines were not being met. Errors were showing up in her work, one of which was costly to the company. Ranton had to take action. This employee expected Ranton to go easy on her because they were friends. According to personnel policies, the employee was to be given an oral warning about her work performance, thereby giving the employee a chance to correct her deficiencies. Ranton talked to the employee, who promised to improve. Things improved for about a week, but then the employee reverted to her old habits. The next step was a written warning that was placed in her personnel file. This warning spelled out the nature of the offenses. It explained that if the employee's job performance could not be brought up to an acceptable level, the employee would be terminated. The employee had to decide whether or not she was willing to bring her performance up to par.

Ethical Issues

A number of values were called into play in this case. Ranton *cared* for the employee both as a subordinate and as a friend. She wanted to be *accountable* for the employee's work to the other employees as well as to her superiors. The employee failed at *promise keeping* when she promised Ranton she would do better and then did not. Ranton had to keep the *excellence* of her department in mind. Ranton had to be *loyal* to her employer and her position of responsibility as well as to the other employees in her department. She had to decide what was *fair* to the problem employee as well as to the other employees, to herself, and to her employer. Ranton's *integrity* would be questioned if she were to show favoritism by bending any rules to favor a particular employee. If she did not address misconduct of this employee, her credibility would suffer in the eyes of all the other employees. Ranton's choice had to demonstrate *respect* for the problem employee's personal problems, respect for those workers who continued to perform well, and respect for those citizens who were suffering because of decline in services due to the problem employee. This was a dilemma of *caring, accountability, loyalty, integrity*, and *fairness*. Ranton cared for her friend but could not let the friendship override the need to be accountable to her superior.

Alternatives

Ranton was torn between loyalty to her friend and loyalty to her supervisor. The employee felt as though Ranton was the friend who had turned into the enemy. She felt that Ranton should not have reported her. However, if Ranton had not reported the poor job performance and the friend had kept making costly errors, then Ranton's job would also have been in jeopardy.

Several alternative actions were possible. Ranton could have looked the other way until another costly mistake occurred, merely delaying formal written action against the employee. If the other employees realized this favoritism was occurring, their morale would have been negatively affected. On the other hand, if Ranton had carried through with written action against the employee, an air of distrust could have arisen among the other employees, which would also have affected morale negatively. This alternative would have maximized caring, loyalty to the problem employee, and promise keeping as was inferred by the problem employee because of the friendship. But this alternative would have minimized fairness to the other employees and Ranton's integrity, accountability, pursuit of excellence, and honesty.

Another alternative was for Ranton to have covered for the employee until her personal problems were solved. Not only would this have meant more work for her, but the other employees would have expected her to do the same for them. Ranton's position would eventually have become a dumping ground for employees' personal problems. Not only would Ranton have overworked herself, but her superiors would have viewed her as a poor manager with little ability to delegate and supervise workers. This alternative would have maximized caring, loyalty, and promise keeping to the problem employee but minimized honesty, fairness, and integrity on Ranton's part.

A third alternative was for Ranton to have continued on her present course of action. She could have filed a written complaint and terminated the employee if an acceptable level of performance was not achieved. This maneuver would have maximized honesty, accountability, pursuit of excellence, fairness, and integrity. It would have minimized caring, promise keeping, and loyalty.

A fourth alternative was for Ranton to have requested that the employee's hours and pay be reduced by five hours a week and that this cut continue until the employee resolved her problems and improved her work performance. If the employee's performance still did not improve by a designated time, she would be terminated. This alternative would have maximized caring, honesty, accountability, promise keeping, pursuit of excellence, loyalty, integrity, and respect for others. It would have minimized fairness to other employees as they took up the slack for the work not completed by the problem employee.

Resolution

Ranton was caught in the middle between being loyal to the organization versus being loyal to a friend. However, Ranton felt that her loyalty rested with the agency. The agency had employed her to do a job for them and she believed she would be doing less than her best by letting this employee not do what was expected of her. She tried to be understanding regarding the employee's personal situation. However, there came a point at which she had to separate her personal life from her job. And Ranton feared she would be setting a precedent she would later regret if she began making exceptions for this one employee. She did not want to harm her friendship but found that when it got in the way, she was willing to jeopardize it. She chose the fourth alternative on the grounds that it preserved as many values as possible yet still demanded better work from the employee. Ranton believed that termination for a long-standing employee was too severe a punishment for her misconduct and that written reprimands did not have the impact that economic sanctions had. This alternative, while sending a message to the problem employee, also told the other employees that misconduct would not be tolerated.

DEALING WITH CLAIMS OF SEXUAL HARASSMENT

Although there are legal remedies for provable charges of sexual harassment, there are far more gray areas surrounding the subject than there are black-and-white (Leap, Holley, and Feild, 1980). That which constitutes sexual harassment ranges from petty innuendoes to sexual insults to unwanted physical contact. Most harassment never reaches the point that it is provable in a court of law. It occurs at times and in ways that are not subject to witnesses who can verify the victim's complaints. The next case demonstrates this.

Case: Handling Sexual Harassment

This is a case of Judy Miller, a newly graduated MBA student on her first job, working directly for the chief operating officer (COO). He took a special liking to the new employee, calling her in for morning chats, pulling his chair close to hers, grabbing her hand, putting his arm around her shoulder, walking snugly by her side, and rubbing against her. She ignored his advances and innuendoes. One day he asked her to drive to a local car repair shop so he could leave his car for repairs and get a ride back to the office with Miller. As she was driving him back to the office, he sat close and kept rubbing her shoulder. When she and he walked into the office together, his shirt was untucked, and when someone made a comment about his appearance and their walking into the office together, he simply grinned and said, "You know how it is."

Ethical Issues

Her ethical dilemma was one of *integrity* and *respect*. By not responding to the COO's "You know how it is" comment, she felt she was giving tacit approval of his behavior. The implied sexual liaison revolved around the COO's lack of respect for the new employee as a competent human being with self-respect. Judy Miller was afraid to anger her new boss, and there was no one higher in the organization to whom she could explain her dilemma.

Alternatives

Miller felt that the COO was taking advantage of her junior status with his sexual innuendoes. She did not know what action she could take without jeopardizing her job or hopes for promotion. She did not want to be labeled as a troublemaker even though she was being asked to work for someone whose behavior bordered on sexual harassment and whom she felt treated her with no respect.

One alternative for Miller was to directly confront her boss. Because she had ignored his advances in the past, he assumed that she did not object to his behavior. If she had quickly stopped the unpleasant interchanges, she might have been able to sustain a working relationship with him. She would have maximized her integrity by standing up for her rights to be respected as an employee and not be seen as a sex object. She would have maximized fairness by giving her boss a chance to resolve the problem without any outside interference. And she would have maximized accountability by being willing to accept the consequences of her actions. However, this alternative carried with it a threat, because Miller had no way of knowing how her boss would react to her confrontation. If he became angry and gave her bad performance evaluations, her record would have been smeared, and it would only have been her word against his about the actual truth behind the negative ratings.

Resolution

Judy Miller's solution was to do nothing about the situation. She was the most junior person on the staff, she had no idea how a complaint would be received or even if any attention would be paid to it, she felt the COO would deny any allegations of making sexual innuendoes, and she did not want to cause trouble for herself this early in her career. She sacrificed her integrity in exchange for job security.

FIRING EMPLOYEES

Firing involves a paradox. It requires caring for and respecting someone while simultaneously taking away their livelihood. Managers typically have little training in how to fire people, and it is one of the most emotionally trying actions the manager will take (Walker, 1987). Good cause for firing is defined as reasonable, job-related grounds for dismissal based on a failure to satisfactorily perform job duties, disruption of the employer's operation, or other legitimate business reasons. Before a firing is warranted, progressive discipline is recommended with rigorous adherence to formal, written guidelines (Howard, 1988). This gives errant employees the opportunity to correct their deficiencies and save their jobs. Additionally, the performance evaluation process should give the employee fair warning that the performance was below acceptable levels. Often it is useful for a third party to review all the facts before a decision to terminate is made in order to make sure the firing is as free of bias as possible.

Case: A Problem of Accountability when Firing Occurs

The case of the liverwurst sandwich serves as an example (Stevens, 1984). When Stevens flew from corporate headquarters to check on Mr. Summers, a district salesman, he arrived at Summers's office at 2 P.M. Stevens was told that Summers was out to lunch. His desk was piled high with papers and unanswered telephone messages. After about thirty minutes, Mr. Summers's secretary informed Stevens that Summers had gone home to care for a sick wife. By talking to a few people, Stevens soon learned that Mr. Summers's problem was not a sick wife, but having three or four martinis at lunch. Upon returning to the office after his prolonged lunches, Summers would turn the place into an uproar, insulting the clerical staff and refusing to talk about business. The only positive factor was that clients really liked him and thought he did an excellent job. When Stevens confronted Summers, he agreed he had a drinking problem. He promised he would reform—and for the next few months he showed he had meant it. Stevens submitted a report stating that although Summers had a problem, the clients thought highly of him, he had excellent experience, and he showed promise of rehabilitating himself quickly. Stevens thought he was salvageable.

Strong supervisors act as a linking pin, tying their subordinates to the rest of the organization. Stevens believed that he was playing a constructive role by being loyal to Summers while he gave him a chance to overcome his drinking problem. All went well for several months until Mr. Summers reverted to his old ways. One day he had several martinis at lunch with two members of the staff. He then told his subordinate, Harry Conners, who had only been with him for a few weeks, that instead of returning to the office, the three of them were going to play cards at Conners's house. At Conners's house Summers decided he was hungry for a liverwurst sandwich and told Conners's wife to fix him one. When she replied that she had no liverwurst on hand, he told her to go out and buy some. She told him that would be too much trouble, but offered to make a ham sandwich instead. Summers turned to Conners and said, "In that case, Conners, you are fired." That night the president of the company received a phone call from Conners's wife saying that she did not think it was fair for her husband to be fired because she did not have liverwurst on hand to make a sandwich for Summers. Summers was fired the next day.

Ethical Issues

In an attempt to be fair to Summers, Stevens had given him the chance to rid himself of his drinking problems. This was in the best interest of the organization since Summers had a positive rapport with clients and a good knowledge of his work, and wanted to stay with the company. But the gamble on *honesty, accountability*, and *pursuit of excellence* did not pay off. Summers reverted to his old ways and caused problems that ultimately resulted in his dismissal.

Alternatives

Stevens could have chosen to give Summers another chance by demanding an apology for having erroneously fired Conners and/or he could have chosen to give Summers a prolonged suspension without pay while he underwent rehabilitation. These actions would have promoted caring for Summers but minimized the honesty that Stevens expected from Summers.

Resolution

Caring for others was maximized by giving Summers the benefit of the doubt and allowing him the time to rid himself of his drinking problem. Excellence was forsaken temporarily because customer reports showed that when Summers worked, his performance was good. It originally seemed to Stevens that it was a fair trade-off to exchange suboptimal performance for a short while, trusting that Summers would overcome his problems and become productive again. The gamble did not work, though.

GIVING REFERENCES

Giving references involves questions of honesty and sometimes promise keeping. The reference-checking system in the United States has become dangerously close to worthless because more and more employers are reluctant to give honest information about prior employees. Often the only meaningful information is whether the candidate is eligible for rehire. If told no, and the company does not have a policy that prohibits rehiring people, then the chances are good that there has been a problem with this person. This may protect the employee who has a bad record, but it punishes those who are good because no one is allowed to tell his or her story.

Protecting the privacy of job applicants, employees, and former employees is important. The collection, maintenance, and dissemination of information to assist the selection and training of employees and to determine promotions and layoffs can endanger employees when used by those who do not have the best interests of the employee in mind. When an employer who knows a former employee well is asked for a personal reference, a decision must be made about how much to divulge.

There is a conflict of interest between the individual's right to privacy and the employer's knowledge of the person and his or her responsibility to be honest. Withholding information from others or distorting information betrays those who are expecting an honest response. There are multiple stakeholders in the results of any decision, and it is important to consider all of them. If one prides oneself on integrity, then one must be true to one's beliefs. If one values honesty, then it is wrong to give misleading information about someone or to withhold information. If one values promise keeping, then one is obligated not to divulge information one has promised to withhold.

Case: The Problem of Promise Keeping

Dan Katchet, a small business owner, learned that one of his former employees was applying for a job with a nearby firm. Katchet received a call asking for information about the job applicant from the firm's owner, who was a good friend and golfing buddy of Katchet's.

The job applicant, Sue Hardy, was a conscientious employee who had always been on time and done good work for the first five years she worked for Katchet. During the past year, however, she had started calling in sick on Mondays, and her error rate had increased phenomenally. Additionally, those who had worked close to her reported that she had become moody and difficult to be around. When Katchet had counseled her about the problems with her work, she had confided in him that she was undergoing serious marital problems stemming from a drinking problem she had developed following the death of her child two years earlier. (This employee had only confided in Katchet after he had given her his word he would not tell anyone about her problems.) The employee's behavior deteriorated so badly that Katchet finally asked her to resign rather than be fired.

Ethical Issues

This was a dilemma concerning Katchet's keeping his *promise* to the employee not to tell anyone about her problems and at the same time being *accountable* to a fellow employer and a personal friend. If he lied and reported that the employee's performance had been satisfactory, his golfing buddy would have had cause to accuse him of not being *honest*. To tell the truth to the inquirer was to betray a promise Katchet had made to his former employee. To say nothing except that the employee left of her own volition was to mislead the inquirer.

There are two commitments and two levels of commitment here. Katchet's friend might not have been able to satisfy his own *pursuit of excellence* if Katchet withheld information about Hardy's weak work performance over the past year. Retaining his *loyalty* to Hardy might have affected his personal friendship with his golfing buddy and betrayed the trust they had in one another.

Alternatives

There is not a clear-cut solution to this dilemma. Katchet had to forsake either honesty or accountability. One compromise was to tell the friend that the employee had not been as productive in the last year of her employment as in the earlier years. But that is the same thing as saying she was not a productive worker, and would have led to more questions or damning her with faint praise.

Katchet could have followed a standard protective practice and asked that his friend provide a signed release from Hardy before he divulged information pertaining to her work performance. The release would have given Katchet permission to give a frank description of her work performance and alleviated the problem of his violating his promise to Hardy. If Katchet kept his promise to Hardy and did not discuss her problems and termination, he would have violated his commitments to his friend.

Resolution

Katchet decided to betray his promises to the former employee and explain her work history while she was employed by his firm. This compromised his promise to the former employee in exchange for being honest with his friend.

The dilemma in the prior case is compounded when personal obligations are included in the decision calculus. With a few hypothetical twists, the next case shows how.

Case: The Problem of Integrity

In this case the caller, rather than being a personal friend of Katchet's, was someone he detested. In fact, the caller, Joe Dotson, had beaten Katchet for the job Dotson now had, even though Katchet was still sure he could have been doing a better job of running Dotson's office than Dotson was. And the circumstances of the ex-employee were somewhat different. Marge Keller had worked in Katchet's office for six years and, in many peoples' minds, had not done an honest day's work even on those days when she was at her desk all day, which were rare. She had always received marginal performance evaluations from her immediate supervisor. Her supervisor had counseled her repeatedly, and Katchet had gone so far as to give Keller days off without docking her vacation or sick leave while she received drug rehabilitation on several different occasions. Katchet had always defended her work to her immediate supervisors and insisted that her work could improve if she were to receive proper supervisory guidance. Unbeknownst to the others in the office (although suspected), Katchet had had an affair with this employee that lasted for the first five and a half years of her employment. Only when Katchet refused to leave his wife to marry the employee did she decide to leave the agency. Katchet felt guilty about having led her on for so long, but he simply could not bring himself to leave his wife. When the employee (and ex-lover) submitted her resignation, she told Katchet privately that if he gave her a bad recommendation, she would make sure that his wife learned of the affair in sordid detail. He had to decide how to describe the kind of employee this person was and whether he would recommend that Dotson hire her.

Ethical Issues

Now the dilemma takes on questions of personal *integrity*. This is an example of how slippage muddies already murky ethical waters. Once an ethical breach occurs, in this case the office affair, acts that follow slip further and further away from the behavior of which one can be proudest.

Alternatives

It was tempting for Katchet to tell Dotson that Ms. Keller was an excellent performer. This would have pleased the ex-lover and saved Katchet from the threat of his wife's learning about the affair, and if Dotson hired the applicant, it would probably have caused Dotson's judgment to look as bad as Katchet thought it was anyway. On the other hand, to have told the truth to Dotson would have helped out someone he detested and caused Katchet to fall prey to the blackmail threat.

Resolution

Katchet decided to mislead Dotson. He said Ms. Keller had been a satisfactory employee and was eligible for rehire. He also decided to tell his wife about the affair in order to prevent further blackmail threats. He exchanged honesty and accountability with Dotson for an attempt to maintain his integrity by admitting the secret affair to his wife.

SUMMARY

Most interpersonal issues do not involve the sensational and the popular. They involve the everyday decisions that affect others in fairly ordinary, but important, ways. Mandatory drug testing and lie detector tests receive a lot of attention because they appear to be direct infringements on personal liberty. As problematic as these questions are from a constitutional standpoint, they are not nearly as pervasive as the kinds of routine situations that have been described in the cases in this chapter.

The cases presented covered a sampling of the dilemmas that arise in the workplace as people interact with one another. These interactions involve informal conversations, hiring and firing, performance appraisal, sexual harassment, supervising, and dealing with peers, subordinates, and superiors. All ten core values are covered by the scenarios presented in the cases. In no case could the resolution maximize all the ethical values included in the problem. Compromises were required. Ethical decision making is difficult because it requires one to weigh all the values at stake and then decide which to promote and which to overlook. Giving up a "good" is hard to do—that is why ethical decisions are not easily made.

4

Conflicts of Interest

Conflicts of interest are problematic not because they are themselves unethical, but because they may lead to conduct that is unethical. It may be difficult to do what obligation requires when important personal interests seem to point in a different direction.
—Robert F. Bruner and Lynn S. Paine

CONFLICTING COMMITMENTS AND OBLIGATIONS

Conflicts of interest manifest themselves as conflicts of commitment or conflicts of obligation. Conflicts of commitment result from internally motivated dedication, or commitment, to a particular party. Conflicts of obligation result from externally motivated dedication, or obligation, to a particular party. Inherent within conflicts of interest is the acknowledgment that one is committed to promoting the interests of one party over another.

Conflicts of commitment force people to choose between promoting the interests of the employer or promoting someone else's interests. They give rise to padding expense vouchers or otherwise showing commitment not to one's employer but to someone else, including oneself. Conflicts of commitment are problematic because they imply that one will choose between the best interests of one party over those of another.

Conflicts of obligation emphasize the fidelity that one party owes to another above and beyond any other consideration. They are conflicts that force people to choose between loyalty to their employer or loyalty to someone else, such as their family, friends, or themselves.

There is only a fine line between conflicts of commitment and conflicts of obligation. Functionally, they produce the same ethical bind, so they are treated as one class and called conflicts of interest. The conflict is over one's looking out for the best interest of one party at the expense of another party. Conflicts of interest pose a threat to one's integrity by leading to decisions in which there exists the possibility that an abuse of trust will occur.

Conflicts of interest are situations in which there is no middle ground that allows a person to compromise both extremes of interest. There is a substantial difference between conflicting interests and conflicts of interest. Conflicting interests connotes the fact that those who are interested in a situation have different viewpoints and different things to gain from whichever action is taken. To this extent, it is synonymous with conflict of interest. But conflicting interests connotes further that there is a possibility of reconciling the differences on some common ground. Conflicts of interest refer to those dilemmas that force a person to choose between diametrically opposed interests, whether the interests are related to personal, employment, or social affairs. There is no common ground that will satisfy both simultaneously.

There is a general consensus about what kinds of situations constitute conflicts of interest. The following three are usually cited by employers as conflicts of interest on the part of employees: (1) any financial investment in a concern with which the company does business, such as a supplier, customer, or distributor, when the investment is made by, or on behalf of, an individual who may stand to gain personally from the action by influencing the nature or volume of the organization's transactions with that concern; (2) the acceptance of gifts, entertainment, or other favors that might place an individual under obligation to someone with whom the company does business; (3) the use of one's official position or of privileged information in a way that might result in personal gain (Adam, 1963).

Conflicts of interest are easier to discuss in general than they are to identify specifically. Within the same organization, there are actions that a purchasing agent may not take that a research director, for example, might very properly take. Several actions on the part of the employer help to prevent serious conflict of interest dilemmas:

a. Develop a corporate policy that is easy to understand and put it in writing.

b. Appoint a company "ethicist" who will serve as a resource person to answer specific questions as they relate to ethical dilemmas.

c. Keep everyone in the company informed and up-to-date about the company ethics policy as it relates to specific cases.

d. Monitor competitive bidding.

e. Study the pattern of purchases and conduct regular internal audits.

f. Rotate people in sensitive areas where conflicts of interest are likely to occur.

g. Enforce the established policies

EXAMPLES OF CONFLICTS OF INTEREST

The cases presented in this chapter focus not on those conflicts that are unlawful and therefore receive the most attention in the public eye, such as embezzlement, bribes, and payoffs. Nor do they focus on corruption, which is official wrongdoing for private advantage for oneself or one's family or friends. These actions are violations of law. Laws are legal sanctions that have been developed, agreed upon, and officially legislated after serious breaches have been identified enough times that elected officials agree such actions should be categorically prevented. Laws mark the fact that a breakdown of ethics occurred, rather than representing the highest manifestation of ethics (Hanson and Solomon, 1982).

This chapter focuses on those conflicts that are within the gray area of ethical behavior, that is, neither unlawful nor ethically obvious. The following behaviors fall into this category: padding expense vouchers; giving and accepting gifts; and being loyal to self, family, or friends at the expense of one's employer or vice versa. That is, they deal with the types of questions that busy people often confront. For example, the following dilemma often confronts salespeople: Evidence is clear that as competition increases, questionable business practices such as giving gifts and offering kickbacks seems to be a necessary component for doing business (Dubinsky and Ingram, 1984). A company may have a policy of not giving customers free gifts in order to curry favor. But if competition is fierce, the sales representative may feel forced to give a gift to gain favor with the customer and play the game by the same rules competitors use. If it is the only way to close a sale, sales representatives feel forced to engage in a behavior that under other conditions would be forbidden. The sales representatives must choose between upholding company policy and losing a sale, or gaining the upper hand in a race with the competition in order to land a sale. To use gifts to gain a deal benefits the companies in the short run but begins a policy that can become quite costly in the long run in terms of long-term business relationships.

To borrow again from sales examples, should a salesperson ignore a present customer's request for assistance so that time can be saved for calling on a potentially large account? The payoff for landing a new, large account is the immediate benefit of the commission. The payoff for servicing a standing account is to forego the short-term boost of a higher commission in order to earn the long-term gain from maintaining a satisfied customer. As in all conflict-of-interest dilemmas, the person in the center of the conflict is in a win-lose situation in which either choice results in maximizing the interests of one party at the expense of the other party.

If a salesperson is below quota toward the end of the year and has several irate customers requiring service calls that involve extensive time and effort, should he or she service the irate customers and probably not achieve quota? At least the customers would be satisfied and probably retain their loyalty to the company. On the other hand, if the salesperson ignores the angry customers and seeks additional sales to achieve quota, management will be satisfied in the short run, but customers' demands will not, and management's long-range goals will not be met because customer retention will decrease.

People choose to behave as ethically as they can while promoting their personal interests as much as possible. Ethical decision making requires that people evaluate the situation, determine the values to maximize, and then do so. Self-interest plays a big part in dilemmas such as these. At stake are higher sales commissions by recruiting new customers plus the contradictory demand to retain satisfied customers. To the disgruntled customer who had been promised service after sales, the salesperson seems to violate promise keeping.

The following case demonstrates the tension between individual conviction and company goals. A congruence of purpose between the employee and the corporation is impossible to force. Ethical behavior must come not only from the top down, but also from the bottom up, beginning with each individual learning to analyze issues and being willing to make tough choices.

Case: Saying No to a Superior

Jane Bledsoe, a printer, worked for a large manufacturing firm. She was classified as management, not labor. Although in sympathy with unions, she did not belong to one. Her supervisor, an old family friend, had encouraged Bledsoe to apply for the job. He was in charge of the office support services, which included the print shop. He was also very involved in the company's political action committee. The PAC supplied campaign funds to political candidates who supported management's concerns. The PAC was staunchly antiunion, while Bledsoe was adamantly in favor of unions. In fact, during her off-duty hours she worked on political campaigns that actively endorsed unionism. One afternoon the supervisor asked Bledsoe to print some material for the company president. The material to be printed was a flyer for the PAC. It encouraged members to vote for a political candidate in an upcoming political race who opposed everything that Bledsoe supported. She felt she could not, in good conscience, print the material. The supervisor knew what was in the material he had asked Bledsoe to print, and he knew her opinions about the subject matter. Bledsoe was indignant that the supervisor apparently did not respect her convictions. She felt betrayed by him. She realized that he was just doing his job, but she still felt she could not print the material. When she broached the subject with her supervisor, he explained that he had felt that her loyalty to the company and her desire to please others would override her political views.

Ethical Issues

Bledsoe was in a difficult situation because she was faced with the dilemma of being loyal to her convictions or being loyal to the firm that employed her. Competing values were at the forefront of the problem. *Promise keeping* was involved because she was expected to do the work the firm paid her to do unless it was illegal or immoral, and this request was neither. She owed *loyalty* to the firm and her superiors but also to her union friends. Bledsoe's *integrity* was called into question because she wanted to be true to her beliefs. She felt that her supervisor lacked *respect* for her firmly held convictions, yet she understood her supervisor's need to be *accountable* to his boss for getting the work done that he had been asked to do. She wanted to be *honest* about her support of the union yet she realized she should *respect* other's views and that others had a right to make informed decisions about all candidates regardless of whether she agreed with the candidates' political views.

Alternatives

Bledsoe had to decide whether refusing to print the material would compromise her loyalty to the firm or whether printing it would compromise her integrity. Bledsoe's alternatives were (1) to print the material and keep quiet at the expense of her integrity; (2) to print the material and express her concern about it when she delivered it to the supervisor, which would have threatened her integrity but at least allowed her to vent her feelings about it; (3) to express her concerns to the supervisor up front and refuse to print the material, which would have protected her integrity and confronted her supervisor's lack of respect for her convictions but hindered her supervisor's accountability; or (4) to express her concerns and ask the supervisor to get someone else to print the material.

She realized that if she refused to print the work she stood the risk of losing her job. The values that would be maximized by this approach would be her integrity and her loyalty to the union cause. However, she would minimize accountability to her employer by refusing to perform the job requested of her.

Resolution

She chose the fourth alternative, which allowed her to retain her integrity, allowed the supervisor to learn how strongly she felt about printing the material, and still allowed the supervisor time to find someone else to get the job done, thus protecting his accountability. Although the supervisor was not happy about the printer's decision, he accepted it and found someone else to do the work. After a few months, the supervisor began to give Bledsoe additional responsibilities. The supervisor realized her potential and knew that she was loyal to the company, as long as that loyalty did not mandate that she compromise her self-respect.

Accepting a job carries with it an implied consent to promote the purposes of the organization. There is an appropriate space for personal self-interest, but it is a space bounded by job-related obligations. Self-interest includes one's own interests and ambitions. Bledsoe pressed for what she wanted to do and communicated it to her supervisor in a constructive fashion, demonstrating concern for her own integrity and yet communicating respect for her supervisor's need to be accountable.

The appropriateness of management buyouts of investor-owned corporations is often couched in terms of its ethical implications. A management buyout occurs when the management of an investor-owned corporation buys the company from the public (Bruner and Paine, 1988). The ethical dilemma results from the fact that the manager's personal interests are pitted against his or her fiduciary duties to shareholders. Such a buyout offers a manager the opportunity to get rich or, at the least, move from being a salaried employee to an owner. Buyouts offer management the opportunity to increase their salaries by thousands of dollars and their equity stakes by significant proportions (Bruner and Paine, 1988). The ethical dilemma arises from the fact that it is difficult to see how managers who are interested in buying out shareholders will simultaneously serve as fiduciaries of selling shareholders while negotiating on their own behalf as buyers. Shareholders lack confidence in the fairness of the prices they are offered, for they realize that the price is also one that the buyers see as advantageous to their interest.

Conflicts of obligation are often played out when the subject of intellectual property arises. Trade secrets are a common form of intellectual property. Secrecy is the most natural and the earliest known method of protecting the fruits of one's intellectual labors. Contractual restraints, internal policies, and external procedures can protect proprietary data and safeguard the right of key employees to depart for greener pastures (Baram, 1968). Contractual restraints involve employment contracts prior to employment, and restraints against unauthorized disclosure. Internal policies involve formulating company policies for handling intellectual property with trade secret potential, and prohibiting moonlighting and consulting. External procedures include agreements with competitors not to hire each other's key employees, although this has doubtful legal standing.

To resolve conflicts of interest requires drawing the line between personal self-interest and obligation to others. A shorthand way of saying this is that resolving conflicts of interest requires drawing the line between one party and another. Accepting and giving gifts involves such a consideration. Gift giving is a time-honored tradition in many settings, from state visits at the White House to exchanges between local offices. Neither the law nor individual organizations provide clear guidelines. The problem is that giving a gift may be, or may appear to be, an improper attempt to influence another party. Or, it may be simply a gesture of goodwill with no strings attached. The following case demonstrates this quandary.

Case: Accepting Gifts

Bill Trumplit was head of a state employment office. The office space was leased from John Blower, a prominent real estate developer in the city where the office was located. Each Christmas, Mr. Blower would send Bill Trumplit a $100 gift certificate from a local department store. Trumplit liked Blower personally, although he would not count himself among Blower's personal friends. He did not want to offend Blower by refusing to accept the gift certificates when he was unsure himself about the propriety of such action. Trumplit routinely accepted the gift certificates and avoided ethical dilemmas in his own mind by simply throwing the certificates away rather than redeeming them.

As the years progressed, Trumplit began to be concerned about whether he had taken the right action in accepting the first gift. He felt he could not stop accepting each year's gift since he had accepted it in preceding years. He also wondered if the other shoe would fall and Mr. Blower would come into his office one day expecting a favor that Trumplit would feel obligated to fulfill. After all, in Blower's mind, he had been giving, and had been thanked for, each gift certificate he gave to Trumplit. Blower had spent the money for the certificate and whether or not Trumplit redeemed it was Trumplit's choice. Trumplit's concern was that he was beginning to feel that he had unwittingly indebted himself to Mr. Blower.

Ethical Issues

As a public servant, Trumplit was obligated to avoid even the appearance of a conflict of interest between the best interests of the agency and a private landlord. *Loyalty* to the agency, Trumplit's *integrity*, and *responsible citizenship* in terms of guarding the public trust are important values. Trumplit owed loyalty to the agency that employed him and was obligated not to diminish that by developing a personal loyalty to the landowner from whom the agency leased office space. Trumplit wanted to avoid questions of his integrity.

Alternatives

Trumplit had several alternatives. He could have decided to stop accepting gifts from Blower and explained that he was uncomfortable because he felt he was compromising his judgment. To take this action would have maximized responsible citizenship but drawn attention to a conflict that Trumplit did not believe occurred, and he feared it would question Blower's honesty and integrity unnecessarily. He could have continued as he had done for years. This alternative would have prevented "rocking the boat" in the relationship with Blower and would not have questioned his integrity, but it would not have resolved the conflict. Or Trumplit could have continued receiving the certificates and proceeded to exchange them for gifts, as they had been intended all along. Just as with the last alternative, this action would have prevented changing the relationship that had existed between Trumplit and Blower for years, but it would not have resolved the conflict.

Resolution

This is the sort of case in which, when all other analyses failed, Trumplit simply could have asked himself the question: How would this look if it were to be printed on the front page of the newspaper? Most likely, he would have said that it would appear to be a conflict of interest and the certificates should not have been accepted. Responsible citizenship is more important than offending a real estate developer. In reality, Trumplit chose to continue accepting gifts because it was more expedient than trying to explain to Blower that he no longer felt comfortable accepting the gift certificates. He maximized respect for Blower, but minimized responsible citizenship. Did any harm come of it? No. Blower never called upon Trumplit for a favor, and Trumplit never offered a favor. However, Trumplit was promoted a few years later and placed in charge of agency operations. His new duties included leasing office space from property owners around the state. At this point, all he could do was hope it was never revealed that he had accepted gifts from Blower in the past.

This case is reminiscent of the gift-giving problem described in chapter 2. The question in that case was whether cultural differences or practices should be taken into consideration when evaluating ethical implications of a specific interaction. Reminiscent of the case of John Donohue and gift giving and receiving among U.S. military advisors in Korea and their Korean counterparts, customs that are taken for granted in one culture are viewed as unethical in another. Even within the same culture, customs that are taken for granted and have become tradition but which give the appearance of engendering a conflict of interest are problematic. To change the tradition that has become an institutionalized routine may engender more disharmony than continuing the harmless practice, despite its appearance. On the other hand, to continue it despite the obviousness of the conflict gives the appearance of being inattentive to ethical standards. This is the point where all values must be compared. Is caring for others, and caring about what is important to them, more important than rigidly adhering to policies that have been honored in the breach for some time? There is not one right answer to this question. All sides of the issue must be weighed and balanced against one another.

Expectations of governmental employees at the federal, state, or local levels are more stringent than for those engaged in private business. This is because public employees are expected to be exemplars of responsible citizenship. Public employees are expected to avoid even the appearance of impropriety. Their behavior must withstand the scrutiny of any citizen who inquires into it, unlike that of private sector employees, who have the right to have their privacy respected unless they have breached a law. In fact, many communities print the salaries of public employees annually in the local newspaper. Openness of all transactions are required by law to ensure accountability for actions. Laws promoting ethics in government focus primarily on conflict of interest, to the exclusion of other ethical breaches, since conflicts of interest can be defined in terms of potential financial gain for the suspect.

Two federal conflict-of-interest statutes impose restrictions on the activities of former federal employees (18 U.S.C. 207) and prohibit current federal employees from participating in matters in which they have a financial interest (18 U.S.C. 208). These laws provide for a lifetime restriction on representing anyone before the government on matters in which the former employee had been "personally and substantially" involved; a two-year restriction on representing anyone in connection with a matter that was actually pending under a former employee's official responsibility within one year before the employee left that job; and a two-year restriction on a former senior official's personal presence before the federal government on a matter in which he had been "personally and substantially involved." There is also a one-year restriction on a senior official's representation of anyone on any matter pending before his former agency or on any matter in which his former agency had a direct and substantial interest (Tolchin, 1986). The Office of Federal Procurement Policy Act Amendments of 1988 stiffened prohibitions against federal employees leaving government employment and going to work for suppliers and contractors. The prohibitions became so strict that many employees left their government jobs prior to the bill's enactment to avoid having to adhere to such rigid postemployment restrictions.

The U.S. General Accounting Office (GAO) issued a report in 1988 of ten Office of Inspector Generals (OIGs). The offices reviewed were the Department of Veterans Affairs; U.S. Postal Service; Small Business Administration; Departments of Housing and Urban Development, Transportation, and Commerce; Agency for International Development; Equal Employment Opportunity Commission; General Services Administration; and the Tennessee Valley Authority. Of 304 reports received by these OIGs, 270 resulted in an investigation being completed, 114 were believed to involve a crime, 124 were referred to the Justice Department, 2 were prosecuted by the Justice Department, 1 was convicted, and 22 involved cases in which the agency took administrative action. The allegations most commonly involved possible violations of 18 U.S.C. 208, which essentially prohibits federal employees from acting in any matter in which they have a financial interest.

In its report the GAO explained that there is great difficulty in prosecuting conflict-of-interest cases as felonies, as is required by most statutes (U.S. GAO, 1987). Officials responsible for investigating charges of ethics violations believe that juries will not return felony convictions on most conflict-of-interest cases. Because of this, prosecutors in both the Public Integrity Section and the Office of the U.S. Attorney for the District of Columbia are reluctant to accept such cases for prosecution, even though they recognize that their reluctance to prosecute deters inspector generals from fully investigating such allegations and referring them to the Justice Department.

Regardless of legal prohibitions, the opportunity to enjoy financial gain is tempting. Some employees find themselves in a conflict of interest as a result of activities related to dual job duties. The next case demonstrates this.

Case: The Dual Roles of Coroner and Funeral Director

This is a case for which the Alabama State Ethics Commission was asked to issue an opinion. It deals with the practice of a county coroner (Alabama State Ethics Commission, 1983). The coroner was part-owner of a funeral home. When called to the scene of a death, he used a funeral home van clearly marked with the funeral home name plates, but the van had a stick-on sign marked Coroner that was attached to the side of the van. After loading the remains of the deceased in the van, the coroner transported the body to the funeral home rather than to the county hospital, which operated a morgue. Upon determining the identity of the deceased, the coroner informed the next of kin and recommended that the family members permit his funeral home to handle the final arrangements. The wife of the police chief was employed as a secretary in the funeral home with which the coroner was associated. Ambulance service in this town was provided by the city police department under the control of the police chief. Often, the city ambulance arrived at the death scene and transported the body to the funeral home of the coroner.

Ethical Issues

The decision reached by the Alabama Ethics Commission was that the coroner should be prohibited from directing that all bodies be handled by his funeral home or transported in his ambulance. Neither the funeral home manager nor ambulance service operator should use the office of coroner to increase the financial gain of their companies. The actions of the coroner resulted in direct financial gain to a business with which he was associated and created a conflict between his private interests and his public duties. *Responsible citizenship* overrides *pursuit of excellence* in terms of trying to achieve more business revenue and higher profits. Furthermore, *loyalty* to the public overrides loyalty to one's own business.

Alternatives

An alternative is necessary to the usual procedure in small towns of the coroner also being a funeral director. A coroner could be prohibited from gaining financially in the funeral business. Or a coroner could be required to travel in a vehicle separate from that owned by his place of business. It could be required that all bodies be carried to the morgue at the local hospital, and that a person not connected to the local funeral home be required to contact the next of kin and ask about preferred funeral arrangements.

Resolution

All governmental officials have some discretion. The question is, what are the appropriate standards for the exercise of this discretion? Both legislative and executive judgment ought to reflect the will of the people in accord with democratic values that promote equality, participation, and accountability of officials who hold the public trust

The next case is a variation on a similar theme. A public employee owns rental property and must decide whether or not to lease it to a subordinate.

Case: The Supervisor as Landlord

Al Small was the director of the city public works department. He owned several rental homes in the city as a personal investment. When one of them became vacant, one of Small's staff members expressed a desire to rent it. The city attorney advised Small that a conflict of interest would not exist according to the city's ordinances or state statutes. Small was concerned about the appearance of impropriety, however.

Ethical Issues

In fact, Small was right to worry. If the employee were late in making payment or damaged the property through carelessness, Small would have had difficulty evaluating him on his job performance without regard for his poor performance as a tenant. Furthermore, Small would have benefited from the connections he developed as a public employee in a way that would help him personally. *Responsible citizenship* holds public employees to a moral standard higher than that to which employees in private business are held. While not violating any legal requirements of the city or state, Small could have been viewed by others in his community or agency as being in a conflict of interest because he would have been deriving an economic benefit from the rent payments made by one of his subordinates.

If Small had rented the property to a subordinate, he would have taken the risk of not remaining impartial in his decisions regarding that employee, which is not *fair* to that employee or any of the others whom Small supervised. From the perspective of the subordinate, *pursuit of excellence* and *loyalty* enter the picture. If a difficult decision arose, the subordinate might have felt unduly pressured to agree with his boss/landlord when, under other circumstances, the decision would have been otherwise. On the other hand, under fair housing regulations, the subordinate might have felt that he was treated unfairly if he were not allowed to rent from his boss.

Alternatives

One alternative is that the supervisor could have distanced himself from the rental business by placing his rental property with a realty company that would handle all rental transactions. By distancing himself from the rental business, he would have had only an arm's length transaction with renters. This would have allowed him to continue his financial interests in the property but removed him from interacting directly with renters. It would not have removed the appearance of a conflict of interest, however. Another alternative would have been to refuse to rent to anyone working under his supervision or likely to work under his supervision. This would have removed even the appearance of a conflict of interest but also cut down on the number of potential renters interested in his property.

Resolution

The supervisor chose to refuse to rent to anyone who worked within the same agency he did. Although he lost some rental business by this solution, he removed any threat of a conflict of interest or even the appearance of a conflict of interest.

The following case presents a dilemma that is frequently encountered by those who travel on business. Per diem reimbursement rates often fail to cover all incurred expenses in some locales, while it overcompensates for costs in less expensive areas.

Case: Padding Expense Vouchers

The following situation occurred in a military organization whose primary function was to advise Army Reserve and National Guard units.

The advisors assigned to the organization spent approximately four days each week visiting client units. Travel expenses were reimbursed based on vouchers filed by the advisor after each trip. By regulation, expenses were limited to those actually incurred on the specific trip covered by the voucher. However, there was a maximum daily limit that varied with the city that was visited, so that one might have a daily limit of $65 in one city and $95 in another city.

The situation involved two officers of equal rank. They were assigned to the same team and often traveled together. For Major Jones, rules were rules and he believed it was one's duty to follow them to the letter. Major Britton considered himself to be a loyal and law-abiding citizen, but he saw no harm in following the spirit of the law rather than the letter if it was to his advantage to do so and no significant harm would come to anyone.

In contrast, Major Jones's travel vouchers were always precisely accurate. If the limit for a city was $85, and his expenses were $76, he filed for $76. This meant that over the long run, he was reimbursed for less than his actual travel expenses, because in some cities the daily limit was too low to cover actual expenses. It also meant that to minimize losses, Major Jones often stayed at hotels that were located far away from the client unit because they charged less than the hotels that were located nearby. This, of course, consumed some additional travel time and reduced the time Major Jones could actually spend with his client. Major Britton's approach was different. He always documented expenses that came close to the maximum daily amount permitted for the particular city he was visiting. Sometimes he inflated meal costs to bring his expenses up to the limit. Also, he routinely stayed at hotels that were next to the client unit so that he could spend the maximum amount of time with them. His justification for these actions was that the army did not expect its officers to have to pay for work-related travel expenses out of their own pockets. He argued that it was acceptable to exaggerate the expenses in "high-limit" areas to make up for expenses from other trips that could not be reimbursed because of lower daily limits elsewhere. He believed that the most important objective was to get the job done.

Ethical Issues

Respect for others, resulting from trust and *honesty*, is violated when conflict-of-interest allegations arise. When one is accused of dishonesty, the news travels fast and strong emotions emerge. Like accusing one of cheating, there is no way to repair the damage done to one's claim of *integrity*. Jones and Britton had to deal with the question of whether it is ever honest to overstate expenses on one trip to compensate for underpayment of expenses on another. Jones believed that strict obedience to the law was the only honest route, while Britton believed that one could still be honest even when the facts were altered at appropriate times.

Alternatives

Major Jones could have disregarded the way Britton filed for reimbursement of expenses. This would have avoided drawing attention to the issue, but it would have sacrificed Jones's belief that pursuit of excellence on the job and honesty and accountability were being sacrificed by Britton. Jones could have filed a complaint against Britton. This would have maximized his interpretation of honesty, accountability, and pursuit of excellence. Or he could have asked for a formal meeting at which clarification would be developed on the correct way to claim expenses. This would have maximized respect for Britton's views but also brought the issues of accountability and honesty before everyone.

Resolution

After one trip together, Major Jones filed a criminal complaint against Major Britton for fraud. Jones alleged that Britton had defrauded the government by filing travel expense vouchers for amounts greater than actual expenses. Major Britton was outraged by this attack on his integrity. He did not consider himself to have done anything wrong. He had not tried to make a profit from his trips. He just insured that he did not lose any money on the "low-limit" trips.

Since the advisor team had only fifteen men, it did not take long for the rumor mill to leak the fact that a charge had been made. Tension grew rapidly. The team became polarized between those who felt that Jones was wrong to press charges and those who shared his conviction that any rule breaking should be reported. Some people who admitted that Britton may have broken the rules still thought Jones was wrong in reporting the fact. They maintained that loyalty to the team should have taken precedence over Jones's inclination to report a minor infraction. Others thought that a less drastic response should have been made. Rather than turning Britton in to the Criminal Investigations Division, they thought Major Jones could have reported his suspicions to the team chief.

The criminal investigation into the incident could not prove that the travel expense had been inflated. It was one person's word against another's, and the hotels and restaurants where the meals were purchased could not identify the specific items ordered by Major Britton and so could neither confirm or disprove that the voucher was in error.

In the end, charges were dropped, but lasting damage was done to the team. The goodwill and spirit of cooperation, which had done so much to make the operations effective, was shattered. It was reestablished only after the two majors were reassigned to other organizations. Work-related incidents such as this do not occur in a vacuum. They involve other people and the trust that is shared, or abused, by colleagues. Productivity of the work group is threatened by problems such as these as people grow leery of working closely with one another, whether or not one is on the "right" side of the ethical issue.

LOOKING OUT FOR FRIENDS AND FAMILY

As a greater number of women pursue business and professional careers, more companies are finding they employ people whose steady date or mate works for suppliers, competitors, clients, or government regulators. The result is that companies and couples face potential conflicts of commitment. The situation has developed so rapidly that few companies have framed formal rules for dealing with it.

Office romances have the potential for presenting multiple conflicts of commitment. Several actions are possible. One is to ignore the relationship and hope it will have no effect on the work atmosphere. A second is to treat the relationship as a conflict of interest and persuade the couple that either the person least essential to the company or both have to leave. A third is to acknowledge the relationship and hope it does not cause problems.

In a case in which a female vice president became involved with the company's chief executive officer (CEO), her friends grew leery of discussing company matters around her. People did not talk to one another because they did not know whom to trust. The female vice president had been one of a group that met regularly to air complaints by grousing to one another at lunch. Whereas before the group could openly complain that "we can't figure this out because the old man doesn't know what the hell he wants," now they fell silent. In the silence, they withheld other information as well, and the organization's informal communications network started going awry (Collins, 1983).

The subject of nepotism is similar to office romances because it interjects favoritism into the work environment. Nepotism must be considered in the light of the company's general policy, the directness or remoteness of the relationship, opportunities for and restriction on advancement as affected by the relationship, and employee relations and company morale in the midst of whispered charges of favoritism. Nepotism results in problems of fidelity. The bottom-line question is to whom the employee will owe loyalty: a family member or the employer? Few employers are convinced the employee will choose them rather than a family member.

Socioeconomic nepotism represents a conflict of interest regarding hiring or promoting someone different who otherwise would be excluded from the position because he or she is "different" from the usual candidates for the position. The conflict is that most people like to be around, and feel most comfortable with, those with whom they have much in common. But this desire runs counter to affirmative action, which encourages hiring job applicants who are of backgrounds that differ from the traditional white male employee. This includes varied ethnic and racial backgrounds, as well as more women. Diverse work forces are difficult to develop because people tend to like to hire people whom they judge to be like themselves.

HE WHO PAYS THE FIDDLER CALLS THE TUNE

Submitting reports as a hired consultant often presents a conflict of obligation. An accountant has several audiences interested in any one audit (Bowie, 1987/88). Although the firm is the client, the firm is composed of multiple audiences, especially the managers and the board of directors. The other major audience is the investing public. If the news is bad, the managers want neither the board nor the public to know; the board wants to know but the board does not want the public to know; and of course the investing public does want to know. And if the bad news cannot be kept secret, the managers want the least disclosure, while the investing public wants the most. How much should the accountant disclose and to whom? The report provides information to the stockholders on how well management is doing. It also provides information to the investing public on how the company as a whole is doing. The interests of the current stockholders and the investing public may or may not coincide. So the interests of the various audiences must be kept in mind.

Accountants must issue report cards on the people and institutions who pay them. The certified public accountant (CPA) is to serve the management, the stockholders, and the general public. Since the interests of at least the general public and the corporation often conflict, the attempt to serve two masters puts the CPA in a conflict of interest. If the news is bad, the managers want neither the board nor the public to know. The board wants to know but does not want the public to know, while the public wants to know. The old adage "he who pays the fiddler calls the tune" is relevant to the situation of the auditor's dilemma. The latter, acting as the fiddler, must still represent the interest of the larger community. If accountants are to perform a public watchdog function, then the CPA must maintain total independence from the client at all times and hold fidelity to the public trust (Bowie, 1987/88).

For example, if the auditor overhears that management is thinking of doing something that might be relevant to the report, but the controller says not to include the information, what should the auditor report? If the auditor insists on putting the information in the report and the deal falls through, management has grounds to sue. If the auditor excludes the information, and if the courts determine that the omitted information was a relevant fact of which the auditor had knowledge, then the auditor can be held personally liable. This is a professional catch–22 in which the auditor must determine to whom loyalty is owed: the firm for which the audit is conducted, the auditor's profession, or the shareholders in the company.

In the past it has been believed that society is better off if the professional-client confidentiality rule is given precedence over society's right to know. Recently we have been rethinking this rule. There is increasing pressure to force psychiatrists to inform authorities if they believe their clients intend to harm someone. Even in the professions where confidentiality has been given priority, there are pressures for change. The questions for auditors are: How hard should you search? What should you disclose? To whom should you disclose it?

Occasionally conflicts of interest arise when an employee is asked to perform two tasks by two coequal bosses and their orders contradict one another. Answering to two masters is a conflict of obligation, and organizations sometimes place employees in the middle of such a conflict. Although matrix structures are excellent for promoting flexibility and interchange of ideas among employees, they often produce severe conflicts for employees who find themselves having to respond to contradictory demands of superiors who are coequal and unyielding. The following case demonstrates this perplexing situation.

Case: Which Boss to Listen To?

The hospital where Betty Friedman was employed has a firm policy for dealing with employees who are caught taking hospital property from the premises. Whether it is the kitchen help taking home leftover food, central supply workers taking home wornout scrubsuits, or nurses taking home medical supplies, the consequences have unfailingly been the same: immediate dismissal for the employee. This same hospital has a very lenient attitude toward the doctors on staff and their actions and desires. The doctors are catered to in a grand fashion because they, of course, supply the hospital with patients.

One Sunday evening Ms. Friedman was alone in the nurses' station on the unit where she was assigned. Everyone else was a few doors down in the conference room having their dinner break. Dr. Dodd, who was a prominent internist and the attending physician for almost half of the patients on Ms. Friedman's unit at any given time, suddenly appeared with a large shopping bag and asked if he could see Ms. Friedman in the storage room where supplies were kept. Once in the room, Dr. Dodd proceeded to tell Ms. Friedman that his mother was ill and incontinent, his wife was upset about the mess in his mother's bedroom, and that he had to get some control over the situation for the night until the next morning when he would see about hiring a home health nurse for his mother. Dr. Dodd asked for a catheter, several packs of mattress pads, and all the adult diapers in the room. Although she hesitated, Ms. Friedman filled the shopping bag for him. When she finished, he told Ms. Friedman that he appreciated her understanding and kindness and that he and his family were indebted for her help. The entire interaction lasted ten minutes. Ms. Friedman felt that Dr. Dodd used her to steal the supplies he needed for his mother from the hospital. He acted on the assumption, Ms. Friedman felt, that she would not object to his taking supplies from the storage room for personal use and that she would not alter their usual physician-nurse relationship, in which she was to be the willing assistant to him when he visited his patients on the unit.

Ms. Friedman was stuck in a no-win situation: when there was discord between a physician and nurse at this hospital and the physician chose to complain, the nurse often found herself without a job or with a lesser position than she previously occupied. She also was not sure how the hospital administration would see the issue. Since physicians, including Dr. Dodd, always donated items to the nursing units, like microwave ovens and coffee makers, she knew there was a chance that, had he wanted the whole supply room, her superiors may have expected her to help him carry it to the car. Third, she knew that the supplies would be inventoried against what had been used and an unexplained shortage would show up. The dilemma left Ms. Friedman wanting to do the right thing and having no clue as to what that was. She felt she had done something dishonest but did not see any alternative.

Ethical Issues

The values in question in this case are *caring* for others, in that Ms. Friedman was concerned about Dr. Dodd's dilemma with his mother. Dr. Dodd's *honesty* at requesting the supplies was questionable. Ms. Friedman knew she, not Dr. Dodd, would be held *accountable* for the missing supplies. She was also concerned about *pursuit of excellence*, since she took pride in being efficient and managing the nursing unit well. She was concerned about whether she should remain *loyal* to Dr. Dodd or to hospital administration.

Alternatives

Ms. Friedman could not be sure whether, if she chose to report Dr. Dodd's request for supplies, hospital administration would retain loyalty to Dodd or to her. If the former were the case, she would forfeit her work assignment, which she enjoyed. She wanted to be fair to Dodd, but expected him to adhere to the same work principles as the nonphysician staff. She did not want to find herself in a situation where her integrity would be questioned and she would be accused of stealing the supplies or allowing them to be stolen.

Resolution

Ms. Friedman chose not to report Dr. Dodd's stealing because she feared he would deny it and she would be the one to suffer punitive action. Instead, she decided that the next time he asked her to give him supplies, she would simply report that she could not do that. If he still chose to take them, he would have to remove them himself.

SUMMARY

The cases in this chapter range from receiving seemingly innocuous gifts to moonlighting as a landlord to padding expense vouchers to having to answer to two bosses' contradictory demands. Each of the cases involves a different situation, but they all hold in common one fact: the situations posed demonstrate a conflict of interest between at least two parties' interests. The resolutions varied from doing nothing to changing procedures altogether to making small adjustments in procedures.

Sorting out what is a conflict of interest can be difficult when one is unaware of how one's personal interests conflict with those of other parties. Self-awareness and being attentive to one's own motives are essential elements in ethical decision making. The great number of conflict-of-interest statutes around the country are examples of the attempt to legislate ethical decision making. It is more effective for individuals to govern themselves and their own behavior than for imprecise laws to govern them. Harsh rules and investigative procedures may cause irreparable damage to company morale and efficiency but still may not instill the quality of decision making necessary to equip staff to independently evaluate conflicts of interest and take the appropriate action.

Policies can be developed, however, and the typical guidelines are to prepare an administrative policy manual; prepare departmental procedure manuals; define limits of authority regarding who may authorize $100 expenditures, who higher, and so forth; and reissue policy statements periodically to emphasize and remind people. Rotation of quality-control inspectors and receiving clerks can also be instituted wherever practical as an added check (Regazzi, 1961).

But in the end, no codes of conduct can foresee all the conflicts of interest personnel will encounter. Equipping staff with the analytic skills to recognize conflicts and assess them in terms of the values involved is the only way to actively promote a meaningful program to ward off potential conflicts of interest throughout the work force.

5

Adapting to Company Norms

Corporate culture is the shared understanding of an organization's employees—how we do things around here. These beliefs, values, norms
and philosophies determine how things work. They define expected standards of behavior, speech, presentation of self and "shoulds."
                                                    —Ellen J. Wallach

Often, personal values are only partially consistent with company values. Adapting to an organization's culture involves reconciling the dis-
parities that exist. The ethical challenge lies in determining the amount
of common ground necessary for both employee and employer to be
able to maximize the values they agree are important without sacrificing
values over which they disagree but which each holds dear.

SOCIALIZATION TO AN ORGANIZATION'S CULTURE

The culture of an organization is defined by its norms, values, and
beliefs. Socialization to the culture is the process of learning about and
internalizing the norms, expectations, and behaviors that are rewarded.
Anticipatory socialization is the term used to describe how people adjust
their beliefs, dress, and personal appearance to accommodate to new
settings even before they enter them.

When a newly hired employee starts work, the other employees determine whether or not the new employee will "fit in." This is not a snap judgment, and they forgive minor indiscretions, attributing them to the fact that the newcomer did not know "the way we do things around here." They wait and give the new employee time to "fit in." Some employees will try to offer a hand in helping the newcomer learn to fit in, without overstepping their understood but unstated boundaries. When newcomers do not adapt after a reasonable length of time, however, they become known as misfits and usually do not stay long.

Culture is communicated through selective recruitment, socialization, training and development, and formal and informal communication channels. The culture establishes a system of norms and informal rules that define how people are to behave and allow personnel to generalize to new situations and act quickly. Even if the situation is new, expectations are clear. Additionally, the culture dictates how employees should interact with one another, how competitors should be treated, and how various departments should relate to one another.

CULTURE AS CONTROL

There are different ways of conceptualizing the function of organizational culture (Lucas, 1987). One way of seeing it is as a negotiated order in which perceptions are framed according to a common understanding. Culture is "order" in the face of turbulence. Structured perceptions provide operational definitions of reality and are used by employees to interpret their situation and act within that definition of the situation. When objectives, rules, procedures, and roles become internalized, the organization can rely on its culture as a control mechanism.

Structured perceptions are models of the real world which ignore much more than they perceive. A company's culture represents a discontinuity from the rest of employees' lives. A company's myths and traditions simplify an unintelligible complexity into an understandable complexity. They provide the illusion of understandability as well as a self-regulatory function for the group.

The higher in rank a person moves, the closer the fit must be between the person and the culture. A hierarchy can be conceptualized as a cone. The higher personnel move up, the closer they come to the apex of power at the top and core of the cone. The lower one is, the more

latitude the employee has between behavior that is acceptable and behavior that reflects the core values of the organization. The stronger a
culture is, the more it reinforces the values and goals of the organization
and extends this understanding to the periphery and base of the cone.
The weaker a culture is, the less it defines the values and goals of the
organization and the less it serves to guide acceptable behavior at the
lower levels of the organization.

For consistent values to be incorporated into the decision-making
processes, they must be institutionalized within an organization's culture. Decision makers choose from among competing norms in order
to put into effect an explicit or implicit set of organizational standards.
A company's history and traditions, its organizational culture and ethos,
its operating and competitive environment, and the preferences of its
key decision makers determine which norms are promoted. These norms
are also incorporated into the decisions of the employees, fused with
standard business practices, and in the case of responsible organizations,
consistent with community standards.

Friends in the company social network provide one another with
comforting explanations of uncomfortable decisions. Those definitions
go unchallenged by those who buy in to the culture. And when unquestioning subordinates have limited contacts with critics outside the
company, they may never be exposed to critical questioning of the
company's customary values and operating procedures. For example,
some cultures treat legal requirements to retain meeting records, to
document files accurately, and to comply with regulations within strict
guidelines as externally mandated annoyances to be obeyed minimally.
Other cultures treat such requirements seriously and demand full-fledged
adherence to them. Since socialization to a culture usually leads to an
unquestioning acceptance of standard practices, employees may find
themselves engaging in activities that they would never agree to outside
the work environment.

An example of how one's work behavior is separate from one's leisure
activities is provided by the difference between lying and bluffing.
Bluffing in negotiations can be a company norm. The important question
is, When is bluffing lying and when is it an acceptable practice? Thomas
Carson, Richard Wokutch, and Kent Murrmann (1982) contend that
presenting false information is lying, not bluffing. But exaggerating
one's position during negotiations is bluffing, not lying. For example,
they contend that bluffing about issues not subject to negotiation, such

as a group's ability to withstand a strike or the union membership's vote on whether or not to go out on strike, is allowable. Presenting false information about issues subject to bargaining such as wages, hours, and conditions of employment, however, is a violation.

ETHICAL CULTURES

An ethical culture is one in which core values are acknowledged and readily discussed in the context of the organization's actions. Caring, honesty, accountability, promise keeping, pursuit of excellence, loyalty, fairness, integrity, respect for others, and responsible citizenship all prevail as much as possible. And yet in the midst of these values is the flexibility and pragmatism to understand that, at any given time, some values must be minimized in order to maximize others.

Corporate social responsibility revolves around the correctness of corporate action, in terms of its products as well as its by-products. The unintended consequences of a corporation's actions are as important as their intended consequences. And responsible citizenship is reflected by making organizational decisions that anticipate and respond to the needs of the community. Ethical cultures are manifested by the relationships and interactions fostered both inside and outside the organization, issues or policy concerns addressed, goals and decision-making processes, and the way organizations conduct their activities.

CONTRADICTORY NORMS

When contradictory messages are given by top management, employees identify double messages and respond to the portion of the message that they assume is more important. Executives may unintentionally encourage their subordinates to commit crimes on the job by price fixing, illegally dumping chemicals, offering bribes and kickbacks, or padding bills. Subordinates do these things because they misinterpret their superiors' instructions and assume they will be protected if caught.

People tend to believe that business norms are different from everyday norms, so when they are asked to do something that goes against their personal beliefs, they assume that this must be a normal business practice. And they may believe that if they do not do what is asked of them, they may lose their jobs. M. David Ermann (1986) lists several ways that a manager can avoid even unintentionally encouraging ethical breaches:

1. Remind employees that not just profit making, but making a profit the right way is the most important goal.
2. Make sure the employee comes into contact with the people whom they might injure by being unethical. An employee who relocates frequently may not be as hesitant about dumping chemicals in a river as one who lives in the area and plans to enjoy the river for family outings.
3. Establish moderate punishments. These, if they are applied consistently, will have a greater effect than extremely harsh but rarely used punishments.

If company enforcement of policies is not likely, strongly worded policy statements that condemn violations and promise punishment are interpreted by employees in the same way that driver's license applicants answer speed limit questions correctly, but then drive with the knowledge that highway patrol officers allow five or ten miles per hour above the official limit. "Since a typical firm has elaborate auditing procedures to prevent embezzlement, theft, and other offenses against itself, however, but none to deal with crimes that benefit it, subordinates draw the reasonable inference that superiors rarely will seek or discover the latter" (Ermann, 1986, p. 34). The following case demonstrates how double messages are interpreted to the benefit of the company in the short run but to the detriment of the company as well as its employees in the long run.

Case: Fraudulent Reporting

Two managers in the Medicare Claims Division of a large health insurance company were terminated after admitting to falsifying statistical data used in the Medicare reporting requirement for the Contractor Performance Evaluation Program (CPEP). CPEP is used by the federal government to determine the efficiency and effectiveness of Medicare carriers. The Medicare contract was in jeopardy, and its cancellation was averted by the company's termination of the two individuals. The falsification was discovered when two things happened. First, an employee filed a grievance against one manager for harassing clerical employees in order to induce them to "voluntarily" work overtime hours without pay to reduce a backlog of unprocessed claims. Second, during a routine review, Medicare auditors detected efforts on the part of both managers to hide documents that reflected unfavorably on the company.

Both of these individuals had held responsible midlevel management positions for a number of years. One had received recognition for her work the previous year when she won the Creative Management Award. She had been selected on the recommendation of the executive vice presidents, and the final selection was made by the chief executive officer of the company. The other manager had only recently been promoted to his current position. His previous position had been in the utilization review area, which investigated fraudulent activities on the part of health care providers as they filed claims for reimbursement.

The company had set an ambitious goal the year prior, saying it would comply with governmental standards during year one and exceed those standards in year two. The ambitiousness of the goal led to a rationalization on the part of the managers that if their misconduct helped the company, then the company would condone it and even protect them if their actions were revealed. However, their ambitions and company loyalty resulted ultimately in their dismissal.

As people throughout the company whispered with one another about the dismissals, a former manager in the Medicare area was overheard to say, "Everyone cheats on the CPEP reports, and anyone who tells you they don't is a liar." Someone else said, "We don't cheat as much as other Medicare carriers, and they are always laughing at us for not cheating."

Ethical Issues

The values involved are *accountability, honesty, pursuit of excellence, loyalty*, and *integrity*. More generally, *responsible citizenship* enters the picture since Medicare is a federally sponsored program paid for by tax dollars. Accountability is relevant because the insurance carrier as well as the managers should be truthfully answerable for any action taken in regard to the contract. Honesty relates to the fact that managers hid materials and falsified statistical data. Pursuit of excellence enters the case because of the insurance company's attempt to meet high goals and maintain high standards. The manager's efforts came to light because of their attempts to be loyal to the company and meet the goals at any cost. The integrity of the managers was at stake because one had falsified the data and the other had made unrealistic demands on employees to work overtime without pay to meet the goal.

Alternatives

The two managers were responding to the goals that had been set by the company. They had a choice of trying to revise the goals downward so they could meet them honestly, choosing simply not to meet them, or lying in order to appear to be meeting the goals. To revise the goals downward would have seemed to threaten the pursuit of excellence, but maximized caring for employees, who would otherwise have had to work overtime against their will and without pay. Simply not meeting the goal would have minimized loyalty to the company and, in the managers' eyes, the pursuit of excellence. On the other hand, it would have maximized honesty. Lying about the data and pushing people to work overtime maximized loyalty to the company but minimized caring for others, integrity, and responsible citizenship.

Resolution

Although it would be easier to condemn the two managers for their actions, the responsibility of their acts has to be shared by higher management, whose subtle double messages created an unfair pressure on personnel. The section manager admitted to the misconduct with the explanation that she had been told by her supervisor to falsify evaluation data that was below par if necessary. She did and attempted to support her fallacious entry by hiding documents from the auditors.

It may be that this apparent fraudulent practice of falsifying records is an industry-wide practice. Regardless, the actions of the employees could result in civil and/or criminal legal sanctions in the future. In order to minimize the likelihood of such sanctions and send a signal that the company would not tolerate such behavior, it chose to dismiss the managers rather than merely reprimand them or demote them. By doing so, the company maximized accountability for its wrongdoing.

The department manager was driven to succeed, and this drive had surfaced in harassment of employees and dishonesty. An alternative should have been available to the manager to secure more employees in order to meet the goals that the company had set or secure reasonable compensation for those hourly employees who were expected to work overtime in order that the company could meet the goals. This would have maximized respect for and fairness to the employees as well as maximized integrity and honesty by meeting the goals that had been set.

Contradictory messages cause problems whether they occur in claims processing departments of insurance companies or in college admissions offices. The discussion that follows shows the dilemma that college admissions officers encounter when they receive mixed messages from college administration on the importance of maintaining high enroll-ments. The situation explains why good admissions officers sometimes make bad decisions.

The world of college admissions has gone through major changes in recent years. Rather than being inundated with applicants as in the past, colleges are now threatened by declining enrollments. This change has placed strong pressures on admissions officers in the competition for students. One question that each college admissions officer must ask when recruiting prospective students is, What type student "fits in" with the current student body? When recruiting, colleges are in the unusual position of marketing their institutions to persons who are both potential consumers as well as products. For this reason, they must be doubly cautious about recruiting students who may not have the qualities needed to do well. When admissions officers are sent to high schools and simply told to "recruit students," this generic instruction may lead to the recruitment of students who are not compatible with the rest of the student body.

Admissions officers must decide whether to lower admission require-ments when there is a decline in the number of applications. By ad-mitting less qualified students, the size of the freshman class remains the same and the admissions office does not have to face the wrath of an angry dean or president. But the short-term gains of having the correct number of new students may cause long-term problems. High school guidance counselors will notice the institution is accepting stu-dents with weaker academic credentials than in previous years and may advise stronger academic students to seek admission elsewhere. The faculty will notice the drop in academic performance among the new students and complain. A higher than normal attrition rate will occur as the less capable students do poorly in class and drop out. The short-term gain of admitting students with weaker credentials is more than offset by the decline in perceived quality by high school guidance counselors, a frustrated faculty, and a high attrition rate.

Another decision chief admissions officers must make comes when selecting personnel to serve as recruiters. Recruiters who zealously pursue numbers will disregard the student's individual needs in their well-rehearsed sales pitch. It is important for them to show the institution in the best possible light and not deliberately expose weaknesses. The salesperson-recruiter is concerned with the product aspect of prospective students, whereas the educator is concerned with the student as consumer as well as product. But those who are too concerned about individual needs disregard the institution's need for numbers, and recruit too few new students.

All three of the above approaches have negative consequences: recruiting students not consistent with the current student body, selling the institution rather than educating the student, or recruiting too few new students. Admissions officers explain their recruitment preferences by developing a logic that justifies the actions. Three frequent rationalizations for these decisions are that the activity is within reasonable ethical and legal limits, that is, it is not "really" illegal or unethical; that the activity is in the school's best interests, that is, that the admissions counselor would somehow be expected to undertake the activity; or that because the activity helps the school, the school will condone it and even protect the person who engages in it (Gellerman, 1986).

The example of admitting students with inferior academic credentials to help meet the yearly admission goals creates significant problems and involves some very serious ethical questions. An admissions officer may feel that it is ethical to lower standards in order to recruit enough students for the freshman class. What this admissions officer sees is the short-term gain of the student and not the agony the student will face in trying to make passing grades.

Second, the admissions officer may believe that admitting weaker academic students is good for the institution because the student's tuition and fees make up a large portion of the school's operating budget. In other words, the admissions officer may feel that by getting the necessary number of students to enroll, the school will stay on sound financial footing. The admissions officer may believe the school set an admissions goal not as a magical number but as a business decision, and that this number must be met in order to keep the school's doors open.

These two situations, insurance claims processing and college admissions, show what happens when values collide (Brown, 1986a). Institutional officers give lip service to fair standards, but the various demands placed on workers to produce outweigh doing what is fair or ethical. Actions speak louder than words, and when employees see the action condoned, they feel protected from any problems their actions may create. It is up to top management to send a clear message to all employees about which values are most important to maximize. Without this understanding on the part of admissions counselors, insurance claims processors, or anyone else in any organization, employees are left to assume what priorities may be.

The next case shows how conflicts of interest can be intertwined, or even produced by, the norms and expectations of a culture.

Case: Coopted by the Company

Here is a situation in which the subject was coopted by the gift of a car loan. It was a conflict of interest with organizational norms in the center of the conflict. The dilemma revolves around a young college graduate, Tim Jenkins, who had been employed with a consulting firm for two years. When he graduated from college he took a job with the firm as a personnel consultant. The firm's largest client was a federal defense agency. Throughout the contract period, the young man noticed that his superior padded his expense account and billed for work that was not completed or, in some cases, not even started. Jenkins had been told that the firm had been given a contract on a noncompetitive basis because it was known to be very good. However, he found a tape in a desk that recorded a conversation between the agency and the firm, telling the firm how to write its proposal to win the contract.

Turnover was high in the firm because staff received little training and were given assignments they did not know how to do, and when they made mistakes they were fired. Jenkins came to see that the firm did poor work, treated its employees miserably, and billed and took money for work not completed. Although he wanted to leave within a few months after he had started, Jenkins stayed at the firm. He had made plans to enter graduate school after he had worked for two years and saved some money. The job paid well, and his boss liked him and often complimented his work. Three months before Jenkins was to resign to go back to school he was in a serious auto accident. His car was demolished and he was badly injured. During his six-week recuperation, his boss and peers visited him often, brought him gifts, and seemed sincerely interested in him. When he was able to return to work, his boss lent him a company car so he would not have to spend his savings on a new car. On Jenkins's last days with the firm, the boss let him know that he viewed Jenkins as an excellent employee and that he would be pleased to give strong recommendations to his future employers.

Jenkins's dilemma came shortly after leaving the firm, when the investigator general from the firm's largest client called to say he was coming to ask him a few questions about his prior employer. The employee knew the firm was unethical and, although glad he had quit to return to school when he did, had made friends at the firm he did not want to "rat" on. He asked himself what he should do.

Ethical Issues

Two of the values at stake are *honesty* and *loyalty*, since Jenkins had to ask himself whether to respond honestly to the investigator's questions. He felt a desire to be loyal to the firm since his colleagues there had been so kind to him during his convalescence. His *integrity* was at stake because he had to choose between telling the truth and forfeiting the good references he had been promised by his former boss. He cared about the *pursuit of excellence* in government contracting and wanted to be a *responsible citizen*. Ultimately he had to decide whether loyalty was more important than telling the truth.

Alternatives

If he told the truth about all he had learned about the firm, he was sure the agency would have discontinued its contracts, and the firm would probably have gone out of business. His friends would have been out of work. On the other hand, if he lied, more dollars would have been spent on slipshod consulting services.

Resolution

He told himself he would answer questions honestly but not provide any more information than absolutely essential. He also decided to call his friends at the firm and tell them of the investigation so they could be forewarned. His resolution was a compromise in which he intended to be moderately honest, forfeit the promised recommendations, and be a responsible citizen. On the other hand, his loyalty to his friends at the firm caused him to contact them and warn them of the investigation and its likely repercussions.

Ethical ambivalence exists when the behaviors, attitudes, and norms that are shaped and maintained by the organization's reward system conflict with the behaviors, attitudes, and norms of individual employees or with the long-term interests of the organization (Jansen and Von Glinow, 1985). Reward systems may inadvertently shape and maintain behaviors that the organization is trying to discourage while punishing or ignoring desired behaviors. Ethical ambivalence typically results from the dialectical interplay between norms and counternorms as discussed in chapter 3. For example, to the norm of openness and candor is the counternorm of stonewalling, keeping secrets, and "playing your cards close to your vest." Tension also develops between some of the dominant norms; for example, openness, honesty, and candor are countermanded by maintaining corporate loyalty. Yet loyalty is challenged when employees circumvent the rules to get the job done (Jansen and Von Glinow, 1985). The irony is that an organization would come to a grinding halt if everyone narrowly followed the rules. There is a need for inconsistency and maneuvering room provided by counternorms. The following case demonstrates this.

Case: Managing by the Book versus by Practicality

A trademark of most bureaucratic organizations is their ability to produce rules and regulations for the workers to follow. The Internal Revenue Service is no different in that respect, for there is no limit to the forms that must be filled out and procedures to be followed. Rod Towlski was a manager in the enforcement division who knew that the trouble with "going by the book" was that he would waste a tremendous amount of time in developing cases for prosecution if he did not use discretion in applying these rules. Not only would his time be wasted but so would his agents' time. This time factor became critical when he was working cases with statute deadlines that if not met would require the closing of criminal investigations. One investigation required documentation of a transaction that had occurred outside of the state. The case was old and already had taken an excessive amount of time. The division attorney had notified Towlski that if the investigation on the case was not completed very soon, the legal department would refuse to handle the case. The reason the attorney had a set deadline was that sufficient time had to be available for the case to be reviewed at all levels and submitted to the United States Attorney's office for indictment prior to when the statute of limitations took effect. The case could not be turned in, though, without this information relating to the transaction.

The procedure manual stated that a formal written request had to be sent to that district where the transaction occurred and officials there would obtain the required information and mail it back. This procedure usually took between thirty and sixty days. If Towlski had followed the required procedure, he stood a good chance of not having the case to counsel by the deadline date. Based on this he contacted the manager in the district where the work needed to be done and arranged to have an agent obtain the required documentation. This was followed up with the formal written request to cover their time spent. Towlski believed his actions were justified even though they violated agency rules because it was in the government's best interest to be able to recommend prosecution on this individual, and no harm would come of the violation.

Ethical Issues

The values involved in this case are *honesty, accountability, pursuit of excellence, loyalty, integrity,* and *responsible citizenship.* Towlski wanted to behave honestly and be accountable for his actions. For this reason, he contacted the investigating jurisdiction by telephone to ask for their cooperation and then sent the paperwork after the fact. He cared about the ultimate goal of his division, which was to identify and catch income tax evaders. He wanted to maintain his integrity and yet do an end run around time consuming procedures. He wanted to be loyal to the agency's policies and procedures, so he secured the required authorization, although it was only a pro forma gesture since he had already received the information he needed. Because Towlski worked for a governmental agency, responsible citizenship was involved; his job was to protect the interests of taxpayers as well as the government.

Alternatives

The consequences of having to follow all rules and regulations is clearly not always in the best interest of the agency or the general public. Workers benefit from parameters to work within so they can treat individual situations as similarly as possible, within reason. These parameters are needed to reduce discriminatory practices that might occur accidentally or intentionally. It is important to realize that no system can establish rules to cover all situations. Employees, whether at the managerial level or below, must have the ability to use discretion when the need arises. At times the stated goals of the bureaucratic organization cannot be reached using the tools that are provided.

If Towlski had chosen to follow the rules exactly as they were written, he would have maximized loyalty to the agency, accountability, and integrity, but minimized the pursuit of excellence and perhaps even responsible citizenship.

Resolution

Towlski's decision not to follow the manual was based on his belief that he had a responsibility to the government and the public to insure that the case was turned in on time. Not following the rules resulted in his being able to accomplish this. The rules he failed to follow were just that: rules, not legal requirements. He made a value decision that outweighed the "correct" decision which, in theory, should have been made.

Towlski had learned that, as long as he could justify his actions, in most cases he would receive the backing of upper management. In this situation he felt that he was successful in handling the situation and felt good that he had not followed the lockstep procedures prescribed in the procedure manual. He would have felt worse about a case lost over an administrative technicality, and he was willing to accept criticism for not following prescribed procedures if it were to come to that. Ironically, situations of this kind happen quite often and become part of the job. One of the keys to being a competent manager is being able to evaluate a set of facts and come to a decision on the best action to take.

PERFORMANCE EVALUATION AND SALARY DECISIONS

Performance appraisal is the process by which an employee's behavior and/or accomplishments for a finite time period are measured and evaluated (Banner and Cooke, 1984). Employees have the right to know what the performance standards are. They need to know what it takes to please the boss, by what criteria they are to be judged, and who will be judging them. It is only fair that employees be informed about which values are most important. If loyalty to the company is more important than being a high performer, then they have a right to know this.

The exchange relationship between employee and employer is balanced when the inducements that the employer offers and the contributions the employee makes are perceived to be equal in value. In an unbalanced exchange, employees see themselves receiving low pay in return for long hours and hard work. In a balanced exchange, employees feel they are receiving inducements that are equal to the contributions they are making to the employer. The importance of assessing balance in exchange relations is that individuals and organizations typically seek equity in exchanges and, other factors being equal, they will withdraw from or renegotiate exchanges that are unbalanced.

The following two cases depict problems that arise when employees' understanding of the norms of the firm differ from the understanding of those who evaluate their performance. "The Problem of Fairness" is a problem that arises when supervisors make arbitrary decisions about performance ratings. "When Budget Cuts Interfere with Rewarding Good Performance" shows another variation of the many difficulties with evaluating employees fairly.

Employee perceptions of equitable treatment have been found to be stronger predictors of absence and turnover than job satisfaction variables (Dittrich and Carrell, 1979). A survey of 158 clerical employees in twenty departments of a large metropolitan-area office was used to obtain perceptions of equity and feelings of job satisfaction. Pay rules and work pace were the most significant fairness elements affecting the expressed satisfaction of employees. Pay rules relate to the fairness of the rules for granting pay increases, and work pace relates to the fairness of the supervisor in maintaining a fair pace of work activity.

Case: The Problem of Fairness

This is the case of Jim Hooker, who was assigned to the telephone unit. In the office where he worked, it was customary to rotate assignments periodically. This resulted in Hooker's assignment to the telephone unit. The unit receives incoming telephone calls and usually involves client complaints and questions. After four months with this unit it was time for his quarterly evaluation. The review would determine the amount of his merit pay increase. As his supervisor went over the various sections of the review sheet, he agreed with her evaluation of his performance until they reached the subject of productivity. Having received high marks in every area so far, he was surprised when he received an average mark in productivity. Hooker questioned his supervisor as to why this mark was given, but her explanation was unacceptable to him. Her explanation was that it was hard to measure productivity in a telephone unit and supervisors had decided to give all workers in this unit an average rating.

It was unacceptable to Hooker that the supervisors used a standard rating for all workers in the unit regardless of their actual production level. If the best rating they could receive was average, where was the incentive to perform better? Word soon reached the other workers in the unit, and they decided to write a letter to the main office to protest this action.

The supervisors responded to the ensuing investigation from the main office by requiring that phone workers do additional paperwork while taking incoming calls. Besides being physically impossible, it was personally insulting to Hooker. The supervisors' action seemed to be in retaliation for protesting to a higher authority. Relations with the supervisors had never really been warm, but this incident created tension between the two sides.

Ethical Issues

This is a dilemma of *honesty* and *fairness*. Hooker and his coworkers felt their work was not evaluated fairly. And they interpreted the added requirement to document their work as a retaliatory move rather than as an *honest* necessity.

Alternatives

Hooker could have chosen to accept his supervisor's rating on productivity. But he strongly believed that the supervisor was not being honest or fair in the evaluation of his productivity. Instead, he insisted on what he thought would be a fair rating. What followed, however, was more unfairness on the part of the supervisor.

Resolution

Hooker's resolution to protest the rating created more unfairness, at least in his mind, than there had been before he protested. Hooker's perception of the performance appraisal process was that it was based on merit. In other words, he believed there should be a direct correlation between the quality of his work and the score on his evaluation. The supervisor believed, on the other hand, that all employees doing the same work should receive the same rating, regardless of the quality of each individual employee's work.

The following case demonstrates how the exigencies of a budget crunch influence performance ratings.

Case: When Budget Cuts Interfere with Rewarding Good Performance

Division Director John Adams was required to complete the performance evaluations of the eight managers who reported directly to him.

These evaluations were due by late December and reflected the performance of the managers as compared to a set of expectations given out at the beginning of the year. Expectations had been jointly discussed and prepared, and periodic performance status reports were given to each manager to provide continuous feedback so they could monitor their progress. Two of the eight managers, Sally Martin and James Bobbert, had done outstanding work and had exceeded their goals. Adams rated them distinguished, which meant they would each receive a bonus in addition to their merit raise. Both were aware of their performance and expected the ratings, along with the salary increase and bonus money. The other managers were fully satisfactory, and would receive pay increases, but no bonus. After the evaluations were completed, Adams was advised by his superior that, because of a budget shortage, the bonus pool had been limited and he would be allowed to give only one bonus, even though he had already rated both Martin and Bobbert as eligible. Adams was instructed to reduce the lower rated of his two distinguished subordinates to the highest level of the fully acceptable rating. Bobbert had been rated slightly lower than Martin, so Adams notified Bobbert of the reduced rating. Bobbert became very angry.

Ethical Issues

This is a dilemma of *accountability, honesty, fairness, promise keeping,* and *pursuit of excellence.* Adams was expected to be accountable for his assessment, and yet when it really mattered, he was informed he could not be. His ratings, which were based on objective performance standards, had to be arbitrarily lowered on Bobbert's record. During the year, the evaluation of performance objectives was explicit and fair and reliable, yet the ultimate rating was capricious.

Alternatives

Since Adams had no recourse for securing adequate bonus monies, he felt he had no alternative. He considered asking the two employees to share the one bonus allotment that was budgeted, but feared that then not only Bobbert but also Martin would feel cheated out of something both felt they deserved. And this would have minimized the pursuit of excellence.

He could have changed the rating to what it was originally and split the bonus between Martin and Bobbert without authorization. This would have maximized caring, promise keeping to subordinates, loyalty, and fairness. But it would have minimized fairness to Martin, who under the superior's order would receive a larger bonus.

He could have simply explained to Bobbert why his rating was lowered, hoping he would understand budget cuts and the need for Adams to follow directives from his superior, which would have maximized caring and honesty to Bobbert. This would have minimized all other values, however.

Another alternative was to have told the superior that he thought an injustice had been done to Bobbert by his having to give him an inaccurate performance rating. He could have sought permission to divide the bonus between Martin and Bobbert in amounts proportional to their original rating. This would have maximized caring, by seeking to correct the injustice; honesty; accountability; promise keeping, in that evaluations would have kept their credibility as reflecting true performance; pursuit of excellence; loyalty; fairness; integrity, by resisting unethical pressures from his superior; and respect for others. It would have minimized fairness to Martin if she had expected a larger bonus, although she may have been willing to share the bonus earmarked for her. This would have maximized caring, loyalty to a coworker, fairness, and respect for others and still not significantly have minimized other values.

Resolution

Adams chose to follow the rules of his superior and give only one bonus award, even though he had already told both Martin and Bobbert that they would receive bonuses. This maximized loyalty to the organization on Adams's part, while it minimized a sense of fairness in the performance appraisal process. It denied the implied promise he had made that they would each receive a bonus, and it denied pursuit of excellence in the long run.

As soon as employees realize that there actually is no payoff for working above and beyond the level of one's peers, or that the rewards promised may not be actually given, morale plummets and productivity goes down.

DETERMINING PRIORITIES

How an organization should work and how it does work are two very different subjects. Broad organizational values are potent only if somebody transforms them into reality. Lofty, abstract principles do not guarantee that managers and employees will agree on how to behave in any given situation. Brown (1986a) says managers' priorities can be learned not by reading the company's code of ethics or policy statements but by observing how they use their time, how they utilize their staff, how they allocate their budget, and how they demonstrate their personal energy.

Values determine what a person considers important while performing the job. Differing sets of priorities highlight value gaps. The first job of managers is to forge a consistency between employees' values and the values of the company. Serious disagreements over priorities threaten morale and cause productivity to plummet. People become more concerned with trying to get along or trying to guess how the manager feels than trying to get their work done. There are three things managers can do to close these value gaps and make sure everyone in the organization is striving for the common goal of achieving the mission of the organization (Brown, 1986b).

1. They can take the official path by quoting policy manuals.
2. They can take the unofficial path by improving policies or using personal discretion for certain policies. This method applies standards on a case-by-case basis.
3. They can take the interpersonal path by utilizing their interpersonal relationships with employees to resolve problems that cannot be solved any other way.

The next case is about charging for overtime when rules are unclear or easily ignored and supervision is slack. A double message is received from the boss: "Do not lie on the overtime report, but we will not look if you do."

Case: Charging for Overtime

At the law firm where Lauren Singleton worked, paralegals received overtime after forty hours had been worked in one week. To receive this overtime, each paralegal had to fill out an overtime slip that reported the amount of overtime worked and have it signed by an attorney. The attorney asked to sign the slip would routinely sign without question. The slip was then submitted to the bookkeeping department and the overtime pay would show up on the next paycheck. It was up to the individual paralegals to see that overtime was charged properly, because no one monitored their time.

When Singleton had started working at the firm, there had been a lot of confusion as to when one was entitled to overtime. The belief among many of the paralegals was that they were entitled to overtime when they had worked longer than eight hours in one day. Singleton remembered when the head of the paralegal committee had told the group that overtime should be billed only after working forty hours in one week. This was the only statement the attorney had made, and he had not provided concrete examples. There was an unstated belief that if the attorney was not going to take the time to clarify this, he could not be serious about it.

Singleton was new to the firm when the "forty hours first" statement had been made. She assumed the statement was a rule and took it more seriously than others did. Therefore, she only billed overtime when she worked more than forty hours in one week, excluding sick days or vacation time. She later discovered that other paralegals were submitting overtime slips for weeks that included a holiday. They may have worked only two hours late on one day of the Fourth of July holiday week, but they would submit an overtime slip for that two hours. Or, they may have taken two hours for a dental appointment on one day, but if they worked ten hours the next day, they would charge two hours to overtime. Singleton wanted to benefit from her peers' more generous interpretation of the overtime rule but did not want to do so until the rule had been clarified by the firm.

Ethical Issues

There were several ethical considerations in this situation. Because the system of submitting overtime did not include anyone checking to make sure that overtime was being correctly charged, the firm had established a system over which paralegals had almost complete control. By not making clear what the policy was for collecting overtime, the firm had created a situation in which paralegals could act in their self-interest by charging more overtime at the expense of the firm. The firm gave the paralegals no incentive to act in the interest of the organization. The values involved are *honesty, accountability, loyalty,* and *fairness.* Singleton wanted to be personally accountable for any claims she made for overtime. And she wanted to file truthful overtime reports. Yet she

wanted to benefit from the overtime reimbursement policy if her peers
were benefiting also.

Alternatives

Singleton saw three alternatives. She could take the high road and
only file for overtime when she knew it was appropriate. This would
maximize her honesty and accountability but would mean she was sacrificing overtime income she saw her peers receiving. Or she could join
the ranks of her peers and file for overtime even when she knew it was
uncalled for. This would minimize honesty and accountability but maximize fairness. Or she could do something about the situation to make
the policy consistent for everyone and also have it serve the best interests
of the firm as well as the paralegals.

Resolution

Singleton asked one of the attorneys what the rule was about overtime.
Singleton's reasoning was, Why should I work forty hours in one week
before charging overtime if no one else does? The attorney advised that
although sick days and personal leave did not count toward a forty-hour
week, vacation time and holidays did count toward a forty-hour week.
It took a while for the attorneys to convince all the members of the
paralegal committee what the policy should be. It was only at a paralegal
meeting several months later that those on the paralegal committee
understood the policy well enough to explain it so everyone would know
exactly what was expected of them. It was after this meeting that the
head of the paralegal committee put the policy in writing. Consistency
and fairness were achieved, and everyone understood exactly what con-
stituted rightful claims for overtime and what did not.

SWIMMING UPSTREAM

Many believe that ethical decay has produced a climate ripe for
corruption. Competitive economic arrangements do not cause people to
become dishonest or treacherous. But they breathe life into preexisting
dispositions to act dishonestly or treacherously. Ethically, "we're all
too close to the edge," one congressional defense aide remarked, explaining that congressional members and defense contractors are in many
ways letting the ethics of contracting slide (*Aviation Week & Space
Technology*, 1988). Contractors have engaged in practices such as bid

rigging and engaging in illicit trade in government-owned documents. Some contractors need certain information and do not seem to care how they get it. On the other hand, members of Congress are known to have called contractors and asked them to pick up the bill for dinner on the town for themselves and their constituents. The constituent believes the member paid for the dinner, but it is really being paid for by a defense contractor. These faults have occurred for several reasons: a huge amount of money and power is associated with weapons buying, contractors are pressured to make campaign contributions to elected officials, the industry often pays honoraria for members of Congress, consulting retainers are paid by contractors, and companies treat certain members to weekends at exotic resorts. Basically both contractors and congressional members are to blame, and the corruption comes from all sides. "Everyone does it," is the common refrain. How can you change organizational norms in an atmosphere of tolerance? Though stakeholders require honest, open reporting, stonewalling and falsification of data may be rewarded. Norms and counternorms are developed. While norms should be ethical and counternorms aberrant, the opposite sometimes develops in organizations.

Organizations are judged by their actions, not their mission statements. Individuals are judged by their decisions, not their shining statements of principle (Cadbury, 1987). Nani Ranken (1987/88) says our actions as managers or workers are still our actions as responsible people. Even a detailed job description does not turn employees into robots. She says the disclaimer used at all levels, "I have to do it this way because it is established policy, but I think it is a bad one and I'm trying to get the higher-ups to change it," illustrates the frequency with which employees at all levels dissociate themselves by verbal disclaimer from policies they consider wrong or foolish.

Being ethical is easier said than done. When one sees a colleague blow the whistle and be reassigned or demoted as a result of having rocked the boat, tough choices remain for thoughtful onlookers. They wonder if they could have mustered the courage to speak up to the power and tradition, which they saw their colleague choose to do. And, even if they could, they wonder if their satisfaction would outweigh the penalties that would befall them. They know that part of their responsibilities involve promise keeping. They wonder if they would have been as responsible a citizen in attempting to uphold important values or whether they have succumbed to local culture, values, and traditions by silence, "looking the other way," or rationalizing wrong acts as being "for the good of the organization and its customers." The burden of accountability, integrity, and peer pressure puts one's ethics to the acid test when faced with cries to "go along with the group," not "be square," or not "fight city hall."

Deciding when personal values clash with corporate norms is a problem many people deal with every day (Wilson, 1983). What does a person do when getting on the fast track to the top of the corporate ladder involves disobeying antitrust laws to improve profit margins? Sometimes compliance with what is right can be counterproductive to the company and going along with what is wrong, if not detected, can profit the company. In each situation, the individual must weigh the options available and determine who will be hurt and who would be helped if a certain option is chosen.

Although quality-control inspectors may want to do excellent work, their performance may be discouraged. For example, pressures to meet production quotas may be transmitted to the quality inspector in the form of orders to relax standards. When there is strong pressure from top management for short-term results, or when a problem is a sleeper that only becomes apparent after prolonged customer use, such as metal fatigue or slow internal corrosion, a question arises about whether to prolong sunken costs or try to address the problem. The ethical problem involves a clash of loyalties between the long-run interests of the company versus short-term profits.

Reconciling incompatible values is one of the most difficult challenges employees meet. When their view of the right concerns and the right way to do a job are incompatible with the generally accepted norms of the culture, the employee can choose to remain and try to change the system, remain and buy in to the predominant values, or leave. The next two cases demonstrate this.

Case: Student Affairs versus Political Affairs

The educational institution where Donald Jones worked was a prestigious state-subsidized military high school and junior college. It obtained more of its budget from tuition and board fees and alumni and private endowment contributions than from state monies. As Jones, the newly arrived dean of students, became more knowledgeable about the inner workings of the institution, particularly the hierarchy, the interpersonal politics, the fiscal base, and the power struggles within and among personalities and groups, he became uncomfortable. Jones's dilemma ultimately involved his having to face the fact that the school routinely engaged in racial, ethnic, and sexual discrimination. As an employee of the school, he was as guilty of the violations as anyone else.

As the dean of students, Jones had administrative responsibilities to the state and to the institution that were, for the most part, compatible. As he became more trusted within the circles of power, he eventually realized the divisions between camps. There was dissension between military staff, academic faculty, and the administration. Confusion flourished between the physical education staff and faculty over which office actually controlled the athletic department. These operational quandaries caused concern among the alumni, the friends and loyalists of the school, and, of course, the employees and their families, who had much at stake and who were directly and emotionally involved in the issues at hand.

Jones gradually realized there was active discrimination against female and minority students unless they were from wealthy families who would make generous donations to the school. Jones came to learn that the civilian directors of the institution were actively giving monetary support to political candidates through both legal and illegal channels. As far as he could prove, no public monies were directly channeled from administrators, staff, or faculty. Indirectly, however, such funding as administrative slush funds and personal expense funds, which were supported by public money, were used to sponsor such political and discriminatory functions.

There were other such incidents in which it became obvious to Jones that the long-term political popularity of the school was seen as more important than the services provided to the students. For example, there were discriminatory policies surrounding the selection criteria for honors students and student government positions.

Ethical Issues

The values involved in this case are *pursuit of excellence, loyalty, integrity*, and *responsible citizenship*. Jones was directly involved with shaping and influencing young people's lives, yet he had to operate for their cooperative education and daily living standards amongst the pressures and headwinds of numerous ethical violations and almost certain although not provable corruption. He was searching for the tenable position and solutions with which he could live. He felt he was compromising his integrity to work in such a system. He wanted to do a good job but could not be satisfied with the criteria the school used to measure his performance. At the same time, he had worked hard to gain his post at this prestigious school and he felt loyal to it and wanted to clean up its operations.

Alternatives

Jones had to determine whether to conform to the school's norms. He decided he had three choices. He could learn to accept the contradictions and work within the system. Or he could remain on the job and try to persuade those in a position of influence to change. Or he could resign. He was caught in a classic exit, voice, or loyalty dilemma. In other words, he had to choose between exiting, voicing his concerns, or remaining loyal to the status quo.

If he had conformed to the status quo, he would have been accepting the school's practices as they were. The only core value he would have been maximizing was loyalty to the school's current administrative practices. The second alternative was to speak up against the injustices. If he were to do this, the school itself would have been harmed because as the problems surfaced in the media, the school's reputation would have been marred. Its graduates would have suffered, its current students would have suffered, and the school would have suffered from smaller enrollments in the future until the furor died down. Jones might also have lost his job if he had brought the problems to the attention of the public. Or he could have resigned his position with the school. This alternative would have maximized his integrity and honesty while minimizing his caring for those who were being discriminated against.

Resolution

Jones coped as well as he could for six years, until the varying and divergent goals simply could no longer coexist on the same campus. He then resigned.

Swimming upstream against the accepted norms of an organization is slow and frustrating, and sometimes even debilitating. And holding values that are contrary to those which one's position requires is frustrating, as the next case attests.

Case: Social Worker Turned Prosecutor

For two years Shirley Wattson was employed by the state's Department of Public Assistance as a social worker in the food stamp program. After the first year, Wattson was promoted to be an agency representative in administrative fraud hearings. This position is similar to that of prosecutor in a criminal proceeding. Proud of her new position, she prepared to present the first case very thoroughly, carefully reviewing the case file and all related documents. Wattson arrived at the hearing to find a frail, elderly woman who was confused as to the nature of the proceedings. During the hearing it was quite apparent that the woman had not committed fraud but rather was a victim of agency incompetence. At the completion of the hearing, Wattson left the office with very mixed emotions. On the one hand, she felt she must remain loyal to the agency; on the other hand, she felt this woman had been victimized by the agency. It was clear that the elderly, frail woman had no intention of committing fraud, but because of Wattson's action, was faced with the possibility of being disqualified from the program for a year. She was in need of food assistance, and her disqualification would be an obvious hardship. Wattson left work that day in emotional turmoil. It was as if the new position that she had dearly wanted forced her to deny her basic value system.

Ethical Issues

The values in this case are *caring, accountability, pursuit of excellence, loyalty, fairness, integrity,* and *responsible citizenship.* Wattson cared about the clients and believed that the agency should do everything it could to provide them with the services for which they were eligible. She also cared about doing a good job, but by being accountable for prosecuting fraud she bore the onus of responsibility for taking away services to clients she believed to be eligible. She wanted to be loyal to the agency and yet fair to clients. In her capacity as an employee of a public agency, she wanted to serve the public as well as possible. She felt she was jeopardizing her integrity when asked to prosecute cases that resulted from apparent misunderstanding rather than purposeful fraud. On the other hand, she had apparently failed to review all the facts in the case prior to the hearing. She had been so proud of her new position that she had failed to make a thorough investigation prior to the hearing. If she had done so, the case could have been dismissed as an agency error.

Alternatives

She felt at odds with the philosophy of the agency. Even though she efficiently carried out the agency's policies, she had very little control over her work. In other words, she felt limited in how much she could assist clients. Wattson felt the actions of the agency were motivated by a draconic pressure from the public and politicians to crack down on fraud. In cases such as these, she felt politics and administration should be kept separate.

If Wattson prosecuted to the letter of the law, she would have minimized caring and integrity but maximized loyalty to the agency. A second alternative was to request reassignment back into the food stamp program as a social worker. This would have minimized her pursuit of excellence in regard to her career aspirations but maximized her caring for clients and her integrity. A third alternative was to seek advice from a supervisor and point out that if this client were found guilty and disqualified from the program for a year, the case could create adverse publicity about the agency and its uncaring practices.

Wattson had brought to the agency a set of social casework values that she was expected to discard in favor of executing "policy." She felt it was wrong to use this woman as a political scapegoat when, in her views at least, the agency had failed in its responsibility to properly explain its regulations. From her vantage point, she believed the agency failed to view clients as individuals with needs and feelings. After this incident Wattson began to look for loopholes in policy, and refused to prosecute many cases the agency believed should have been. The agency began to view her as disloyal, while she believed she was helping the people the agency was charged to serve. In preparing cases for fraud, she started to take the attitude that the agency may have been responsible for its own losses. She began to view her work as unpleasant and the agency as the "bad guy."

Although her empathy for the plight of the elderly woman was genuine, what disturbed her most was her own visibility to the public. As an agency representative she became accountable to the public for the actions of the agency. Her value system became subordinate to agency policy. Executing policy was never a problem when she was relatively anonymous and the client was a case file. But all that changed when she came face-to-face with people she was expected to prosecute.

Resolution

She soon resigned her position and left the agency. She concluded that the norms within the agency were so incompatible with what she thought they should be that she did not want to be affiliated with it in any way.

Professionals who must work together on interdisciplinary teams encounter conflicts not only between themselves and the organization but also between themselves and their teammates who were trained in other disciplines. For example, forensic scientists function within an adversarial system of justice that places a high premium on winning cases. But the professions of science, medicine, and the law make for strange bedfellows. The scientist, as a scientist, is expected to obtain the "right" answer from performing unbiased scientific tests. To the police officer, the only "right" answer is the one that points to the guilt of the defendant. The conflict is made worse by the fact that attorneys are free to interpret scientific evidence in a way that supports their client. Scientists, however, are not supposed to tolerate the arbitrary presentation of data or the deliberate concealment of unfavorable experimental outcomes. For the scientist hired by counsel as an expert witness, compromises are made in what evidence is solicited from the witness at the discretion of the attorney, and this mitigates the scientific purity of the scientist's work (Frankel, 1989; Lucas, 1989; Peterson, 1989). To some who work in forensics, such conflicts are so severe that they choose to change fields of expertise rather than see their values compromised almost daily. Others learn to reconcile their differences to a degree that will permit them to work together. They cling tenaciously only to those values that are absolutely essential for them to feel justified in their work.

SUMMARY

This chapter covers the topic of corporate culture and explains how contradictory norms give rise to unethical behavior and how individuals adapt their personal values to make them compatible with the organization's. Some cases revealed situations in which the employee's values were so contrary to the company's that the employee resigned rather than try to change the system. Another case showed how using contradictory norms actually furthers the responsiveness of the organization. And another showed how, if an individual's values are not consistent enough with those of the organization, the employee will not do well on the job.

The greatest frustration for ethical people who find themselves in unethical cultures is that to change particular behaviors requires changing a set of interrelated cultural norms. To do so is like trying to identify an elephant when one is blindfolded. The trunk feels like a snake, the side feels like a wall, and the leg feels like a tree. The behemoth is too large to be controlled by one person's effort.

Employees come to new jobs with high hopes. Socialization to a positive, constructive set of cultural norms is important during their orientation period. All employees wish to be associated with a set of values that will enhance them individually and reflect positively on their organization (Erdlen, 1979). These norms reflect the ethical premises of the organization. Since first impressions are lasting impressions, the new employee should be welcomed with information that clearly sets forth the ethical standards that are to be practiced.

Constancy is required to establish a continuity of standards. The organization must foster individual reliance so that when an employee says, "It's not my job," someone else immediately replies that protecting the company's reputation is everybody's job. To the statement that "the law doesn't say we have to" must come the counterpoint that moral obligations go beyond the law. To the point that "it's company policy" must come the counterpoint that policies back up ethics, they do not create them.

Organizational development can be used to address many problems in the corporate culture. Ethical problems and dilemmas are the mutual responsibility of both change agents and client systems. One of the biggest stumbling blocks to effective organizational development efforts is determining which set of values will be maximized and which will be minimized. Organizational development must be highly integrative and consider all perspectives to a problem. Lack of clarity concerning goals, values, needs, and change methods can result in poorly defined and poorly understood change effort. When value and goal conflicts are poorly understood at the beginning, the organization development effort will be short lived.

6

Good Citizenship

We often make the mistake of believing that what happens at the bottom
makes no difference. As a matter of fact, it is what we do at the bottom
which decides what eventually happens at the top.

—Eleanor Roosevelt

INDIVIDUAL VERSUS COMMUNITY INTERESTS

Being a good citizen requires that one choose the greater good when
confronted with questions of self-interest versus public interest. As
discussed in chapter 1, Vincent Barry (1979) argues that there are four
ethical standards that can be used to produce ethical behavior. One of
the four applies particularly well to the topic of good citizenship: act
in such a manner that if your act were to be made a general law for
everyone to follow, it would promote general human and social success.
In other words, ask what would happen if everyone did this. If the
answer is that everyone would benefit, then the act passes its ethical
test. The converse of this maxim is that if the results would not be good
for society as a whole, then the action should not be taken.

An essential element of the American way of life is the emphasis on
individual rights. But being a responsible citizen also requires promoting
the interests of the community as a whole. When ethical scrutiny is

applied to the relationship between micromotives and macrobehavior, the tension between individual rights and community welfare becomes obvious (Schelling, 1978). The tragedy of the commons results. This is when each individual exercises individual rights but collectively each person's separate action results in the group's loss. The following examples demonstrate what happens:

- If there is a fire in the theater, each person tries to escape (micromotive). But in the process, all die trying to exit since they all converge on the exit at once and block each individual's exit.

- As people individually choose to congregate with those with whom they feel most comfortable (micromotive), the result in the community is economic, racial, and ethnic segregation of housing, schools, and businesses.

- As each worker wants and receives higher wages, the end result is that products become noncompetitive in the world marketplace because they are too expensive.

- As preferential hiring is practiced to allow previously excluded groups to enter the workplace, the traditionally favored worker ends up being discriminated against.

- As U.S. taxpayers insist on paying fewer taxes but demand more services, the national debt rises due to deficit spending.

Responsible citizenship requires people to draw the line between self-interest and the greater interest of the community at large. The point where people's right to do as they please stops and society's right to inhibit individual actions begins, occurs where one more action on the individual's part will harm more people than it helps.

Good actions by an individual are occasionally sacrificed for the sake of consistency in applying laws the entire community must follow. Some will argue that more flexibility should be applied when laws are being enforced, while others argue that the ends, as good as they may be, do not justify suspending the law. The following case provides an example of this debate. A community-service organization would have benefited from a county law being lifted to allow a one-time purchase of land. But exempting one organization from the law gives rise to many more requests for exemptions.

Case: Getting a Land Permit

Ruth Yoles was the executive director of the Youth Home for Abused Children. After months of searching, she had finally located a suitable, affordable site on which to build a new facility to replace the run-down building currently in use. The land was being offered for sale far below market value at $1,300 per acre. The tract was located off the main road and the roads leading to the property were unpaved. However, the price of the land was so low that even after having to pave the roads, the cost per acre would be only $3,000, which was still below market value.

Since the county funded the youth home, Yoles had to have all large purchases approved through the county commission. When she informed the commissioners of the potential purchase, they reminded her that if she bought only a parcel of this property the seller would be responsible for paving all access roads leading into it. A new law required sellers to pave access roads leading into their property if they were going to sell small tracts of land. The reason for the law was that the county was getting stuck with paving roads because new subdivisions were going up everywhere. The new law took a financial load off the county. Yoles checked and found that the entire property was fifty acres. She could not possibly purchase this much land in order to keep the owner from having to pave all access roads. When the seller was told that he would have to pave all access roads, he refused to sell the tract.

Yoles decided to plead her case before the county commission, county engineer, and county attorney. She was told that the county commission had met and discussed the law earlier in the year. The county engineer had brought information to the commission showing how much money, equipment, and labor were being spent on paving access roads into areas that had become populated. They were becoming populated because landowners were selling off five- to ten-acre tracts of large landholdings; buyers purchasing the land were building homes and wanting their roads paved. The county engineer had argued that it was not the county's responsibility to pave these roads because landowners knew they would become subdivisions and should have paved them prior to selling the property. His arguments had been persuasive, and the commissioners had decided to enforce the law regardless of the situation or circumstances involved.

Yoles was angry with the county's decision. The cost of paving the roads would only bring the cost of the land up to $3,000 per acre. It seemed illogical to refuse the offer when land was selling for $6,000 per acre. Yoles was frustrated because for over a year she had been looking for land and had finally found some her budget could afford, only to receive this response. She could not understand why the commission could not make a special concession for the youth home since all the commissioners agreed a new one should be built as soon as possible at the lowest cost. The county knew that Yoles's present facility flooded two or three times each year and that the house was falling apart. They knew how long she had been looking for land and they knew how much money she could spend. However, they chose not to go against their original decision and make special arrangements for the youth home.

Ethical Issues

The values involved were *accountability, pursuit of excellence, fairness,* and *responsible citizenship.* Yoles was concerned about the facility for which she was responsible. She wanted to provide the best services possible within her budget. She felt it would be fair to waive the road-building law because the services her facility provided were necessary for the county and development of that one parcel would not result in another subdivision being built. She believed the commissioners' decision not to waive the rule was penny-wise and pound-foolish. On the other hand, the commissioners believed that in order to be accountable, they had to enforce the law uniformly and make no exceptions. They believed they would maximize accountability, fairness, and responsible citizenship by not wavering on their resolve.

Alternatives

The obvious alternative in this case was for the commissioners to waive the rule that required sellers to build access roads. Since the purchase was being made for a nonprofit organization that provided services to the youth of the county, the argument could be made that there was sufficient justification for setting aside the rule in this instance.

Resolution

Organizational responsiveness to the community requires that each organization balance its needs and enterprise with the needs of the community. In order to practice good citizenship, the individual is occasionally called upon to subjugate personal short-term interest for the greater good of the group, company, or agency. In this case, Yoles was forced to locate another site for the youth home, which she did. However, she had to pay far more for it than the original site would have cost. In terms of dollars and cents, the county won the battle but lost the war. In terms of setting an example for rigid enforcement of laws, the county won both the battle and the war.

The following case is a variation of the same theme but with more personal implications. Laws are only as just and fair as the judgment of the person enforcing them.

Case: The Adoption Decision

When working as a social worker with the Child Welfare Department, John Doster received a neglect complaint from a child's paternal aunt and uncle. They stated that the child was not being fed and clothed properly and that the mother was too sick to care for the child. The aunt and uncle wanted the child to come and live with them. Doster made a home investigation and found a clean, well-fed, happy child who appeared to love his mother. But he learned that the mother had terminal cancer and had been suffering from depression since the death of her husband in an automobile accident a few months earlier. She told him that the doctors had given her about a year to live and she realized her son needed a permanent home. She had agreed for the aunt and uncle to take custody of her child after her death but said they had become hostile and angry because she insisted that they wait until she died to take full custody. She explained that her brother-in-law and his wife were unable to have children of their own and had always been close to her son. She believed they were good people and that he would enjoy living with them. Their unwillingness to wait, however, had led to angry words between them. They hardly spoke to one another anymore. After talking with all the neighbors and concluding the investigation, Doster reported that the abuse complaint was unfounded.

The aunt and uncle continued to frequent Doster's office, stating that they were going to sue for adoption the next time an incident occurred. They complained that neighbors kept the child during the mother's hospital stays and they believed they should be allowed to keep him instead. Doster tried to persuade them to reestablish their relationship with the mother, but they refused and said they would see her in court.

A few months elapsed, and the mother had a severe bout with depression and more chemotherapy. She was hospitalized for treatment. During this time the aunt and uncle repeated their complaint that the child was being cared for by neighbors and that they, as living relatives, should be keeping the child instead. The aunt hired a psychiatrist to interview the mother in the hospital and he reported that the natural mother was mentally incompetent. The case was presented to a judge in a special hearing and the judge ordered Doster's agency to investigate the aunt and uncle, since they were living relatives willing to take the child. The agency, of course, found the aunt and uncle acceptable, and the child was transferred immediately to their residence.

When the mother finally was released from the hospital Doster had to tell her about the decision that had been made and that her son was now living at her brother-in-law's house. She became upset and said, "Well, they finally got what they wanted. Now they've left me to die." She worried that they would not even want her to visit her son, but Doster assured her that they had to let her visit. He arranged a visit for the next day in his office, and the aunt and uncle brought the child. The mother was right: they were not pleased with this visit and said it was not good for the child to see his mother in her weakened condition and they were going to try and get visits stopped. They began legal proceedings to sue for adoption of the child and terminate the mother's rights.

The mother's condition continued to deteriorate after this episode, and more chemotherapy was required and more depression accompanied it. At the court hearing, the aunt and uncle presented their case for adoption. Doster recommended that the aunt and uncle be granted only temporary custody while the mother was living, so she could continue to see her child, but the judge ruled that the mother was unable to care for the child and was in the hospital the majority of the time. Since the aunt and uncle were willing to adopt the child at this time, that is what the judge ordered. The mother's parental rights were terminated, all contact was stopped, and the aunt and uncle gained full custody of the child. The mother died about six months later.

Ethical Issues

The values involved in this case were *caring, promise keeping, fairness, respect for others,* and *responsible citizenship*. Everyone involved in the case cared about the child's welfare. The disagreements came over how to protect the child's interest and yet respect the rights of the mother. The mother had made a promise to her brother-in-law and his wife that her son would become theirs upon her death, and she never wavered from that promise. The child's aunt and uncle, however, felt they were being treated unfairly when they were denied the right to care for the child during the mother's hospitalizations.

Responsible citizenship enters into child welfare cases because society's interests must be protected in terms of providing the best home life for youth so they will grow up to be responsible citizens. Upholding and interpreting the laws of the land are an essential ingredient of citizenship. Yet protecting the rights of the mother and caring about her agony from having lost a husband in a car accident and watching her life dwindle away could not be ignored.

Alternatives

There were several alternatives for the aunt and uncle in this case. They could have waited patiently for the mother to die, even though they wanted custody of the child sooner. But in their minds, this alternative would have jeopardized the welfare of the child. The judge could have decreed that the mother have custody until her death. This would have maximized respect for her rights as the child's natural mother. Or the aunt and uncle could have tried to make amends with the mother during her last months so that even though they had custody of the child, the mother could have seen the boy frequently. This would have maximized caring and respect for the mother.

Resolution

The judge knew how hard it was to find placements for children and he knew the mother was very ill. He decided that the willingness of the aunt and uncle to adopt the child provided the best alternative for protecting the welfare of the child and for stopping the feud between the mother and her brother-in-law and his wife. He believed that the child needed a stable home environment regardless of the trauma the natural mother would suffer in the process. Since the mother's days were numbered, he decided to focus on the welfare of the child at the expense of the mother's.

Having to decide such an issue results in a tragic choice. Much as deciding who should receive scarce organs for transplants, such decisions require that as one party benefits, the one denied forfeits virtually everything.

Individual Rights versus Community Obligation

A community has an obligation to serve all its residents. But sometimes the obligation runs into opposition from citizens who insist on protecting their individual rights. Providing rehabilitation facilities for a community's handicapped citizens is an example. Finding a suitable site for a halfway house is often a problem. A halfway house provides a sheltered living arrangement for persons who need supervision as they learn to cope with living on their own. Such a facility is usually used as a transition for persons who have been accustomed to a more dependent living situation in an institution or with family members. In order to help them gain the skills necessary to live more independently, they benefit from living for a few months in a halfway house. Many such halfway houses provide services to the mentally ill, mentally retarded, or to parolees.

When a community mental health center, psychiatric facility, or prison tries to establish a halfway house in a neighborhood setting, it runs into opposition from the residents who surround the planned facility. Out of fear, neighbors are afraid for their safety. They fear they will be unable to sell their homes at a fair market price, thus they complain that their property values will drop. Petitions and phone calls flood the offices of elected officials, asking them to oppose the plan.

If an organization or community wants to recommend a halfway house, then, out of respect for the fears of the neighboring residents, it must be prepared to educate the citizens who will be affected by it. The values of fairness, respect for others, and responsible citizenship demand that each side have the right to express their wishes and reservations and hear what others have to say. Communities do themselves a favor when they provide for the rehabilitation of those who have been living in institutions and are capable of reentering the community. On the other hand, communities have an obligation to protect the rights of citizens to own property and protect their investments. To maximize the rights of one group over those of another implies a disregard or minimization of the importance of the losing group's concerns.

PROMOTING DEMOCRATIC VALUES IN THE WORKPLACE

Changes in the American marketplace are happening at a fast pace. As the pressure for higher productivity increases, the labor force comes under closer and closer scrutiny. As wages go up, the cost of manufacturing goes up, and ultimately competitiveness of the product is diminished. Consequently, the cry for higher productivity increases, the demand for higher wages increases, and the vicious cycle continues. Salaries of chief executive officers of large corporations are in multimillion-dollar sums, while the same CEOs declare that wage ceilings for hourly workers are necessary to keep a product marketable. Shortsighted greed threatens to overcome farsighted prudence. This is also apparent from the spate of corporate acquisitions in recent years.

Many stakeholders are affected by mergers and buyouts, including stockholders, creditors, employees, customers, suppliers, competitors, government, and communities. While some stakeholders gain from acquisitions, other stakeholders lose. Capitalism is built upon the assumptions that some businesses will perform better than others and that the best will survive while the poor performers will be bought out, sold, or dissolve. While not denying this fact of life, Robert Cooke and Earl Young (1987/88) pose questions to highlight the involvement of all stakeholders in corporate transitions, even those not immediately involved in the negotiations. They suggest that when these questions are answered before completing a merger or other transaction, the best interests of all stakeholders are more likely to be promoted.

— Are there ways to consolidate or merge that will not have negative consequences for a large number of stakeholders?

— Will each stakeholder be treated with dignity and respect in the merger process?

— If negative effects are unavoidable, are there mechanisms to alleviate or lessen the impact?

— If there are negative consequences, can these be shared among the various stakeholders, so that no individual or group bears the full brunt of the consequences?

— If any stakeholders suffer loss, are there measures that can be taken to alleviate the loss?

Human resources management includes planning, staffing, appraising, compensating, training, and development. These functions promote democratic vaues because affirmative-action guidelines emphasize that recruiting, selecting, compensating, and evaluating employees must be done in a way that maximizes the relevance of job performance and minimizes attention to non-job-related factors such as race, sex, religion, or national origin.

Responsible citizenship requires that corporations act responsibly in promoting the laws of the land. In terms of hiring, all applicants are to be treated equally and fairly. However, the following case shows how personal biases creep into otherwise objective assessment and selection procedures.

Case: Counteracting Biases

This is the case of Linda Smith and Bill Robbins, both assessment center evaluators in the personnel office of a large state agency. Both were aware that prejudice slips into evaluators' judgments as hard as they try not to let it. But neither was aware of how much their biases affected their ratings. Smith was aware that Robbins consistently shaved the scores of what he called "aggressive feminists," whom he believed caused tension in the workplace. Knowing he did this, Smith gave higher scores to this type of person in order to counteract Robbins's lower ratings.

Ethical Issues

Smith was attempting to compensate for the prejudices of her colleague. Was this *honest*? No, it was not. Was it *fair*? Perhaps so, as a means to counterbalance an unwarranted low rating. But actually, neither was being fair because neither was giving honest evaluations. Was it *responsible citizenship?* Yes, it was, because its goal was to promote an unbiased assessment of work characteristics, and one evaluator's unduly low rating was balanced by the other's unduly high rating. Was it an effective way to ensure equal employment opportunity? No. Both Robbins and Smith failed to be *accountable* to the standards provided them as personnel officers and the inherent responsibilities of their positions. This sacrifice, along with that of honesty, provided for a rather shabby *pursuit of excellence*. Having violated fairness, accountability, pursuit of excellence, and honesty, there was little *integrity* left in the process of making evaluations.

Alternatives

Several alternatives were possible. Smith and Robbins could have talked over their differences to see if they could come to common understanding of how ratings were to be applied. The department could have developed an assessment system where ratings were protected from the injection of personal bias. Training and development of evaluators could have included clear-cut specifications for removing bias from the evaluators' judgments.

Resolution

Perhaps the most important issue here is the willingness of one person to take responsibility for correcting abusive practices within the organization. Individual responsibility is an essential ingredient if organizations are to be ethical places to work. Unfortunately, in this case Smith had to take a rather convoluted means to accomplish this. Clear-cut standards that would prevent the injection of Robbins's personal biases would have been a more reliable solution. By failing to insist on unbiased scoring as soon as Smith became aware of Robbins's bias, she compromised her ability to blow the whistle on him later. Once she began to score applicants falsely, her scores were as faulty as Robbins's. Two wrongs do not make a right. She could not correct Robbins's injustice by adding her own.

Responsible citizenship in the U.S. workplace requires promoting democracy within a hierarchy and promoting the right to self-governance to the greatest extent possible. Organizational learning is the process by which personnel detect errors and then correct them through changing company policy. This learning occurs on two levels: single-loop learning and double-loop learning. Managing effectively requires understanding the difference between single-loop and double-loop learning. When walking into a stuffy room, a single-loop response would be, "It is hot, open a window." A double-loop response would be, "It is hot, open a window to solve the immediate problem and adjust the thermostat to solve the long-term problem." Single-loop learning occurs when personnel learn to carry out policies to achieve the organization's goals. Double-loop learning occurs when personnel question underlying policies and goals.

Single-loop learning is practiced more often than double-loop learning in large bureaucracies because each layer in the hierarchy and each department has only a circumscribed set of responsibilities. Few rewards are given to those who want to "rock the boat" by reconsidering basic policies and procedures that have been put in place by those elsewhere in the hierarchy.

Open discussions of policies encourage double-loop learning. Employees throughout large organizations should be encouraged to present their points of view about procedures and objectives (Barth, 1987–88). Otherwise, higher levels of learning do not occur, and the public suffers in the long run.

PRIVACY RIGHTS

Most Americans equate interference in their private lives with the loss of freedom. But modern society necessitates that information of a personal nature be kept by government agencies, credit bureaus, insurance firms, schools, colleges, and the military, as well as many other organizations. Information is needed for tax collection, lending programs, credit checks, welfare programs, retirement benefits, personnel placement, insurance claims, and criminal investigations. Administration of these programs would be impossible without the collection, maintenance, and retrieval of data about personal income, work history, and personal health, and in some cases fingerprints or even individual DNA records. The technology of the second half of the twentieth century has brought the issue of privacy to the forefront. The tax system accumulates almost inconceivable amounts of data from individuals, employers, and banks in order to validate and audit the tax returns of some 200 million individuals and 50 million businesses annually (Internal Revenue Service, 1986). The Social Security Administration also collects information from those individuals and businesses, and maintains additional records on payments to retirees, the disabled, and dependents, as well as investigative files on the qualifications of claimants. The Department of Veterans Affairs as well as several other federal agencies collects and maintains similar records in order to administer their programs, and frequently those records duplicate information maintained by others. Additional duplication exists on both the state and local levels. The duplication exists in large part because the legislation that requires each set of records also requires that the information be kept confidential. Limits are further enforced by such legislation as the Privacy Act of 1974, the Fair Credit Reporting Act of 1970, the Right to Financial Privacy Act of 1978, and various pieces of state legislation (Ellis, 1985).

The key ethical question involved is not whether organizations should maintain information on individuals. Society cannot be maintained as we know it without doing so. The ethical question is how scrupulously an organization will honor the confidentiality of the information.

The arguments in favor of strengthening privacy statutes are persuasive. They seek to prevent the intrusion of government, employers, and regulatory bodies into people's personal lives. Tax data contains information about salaries, bank accounts, stock holdings, business and personal assets, and marital status. Social Security records have similar income information, and also contain data about health and employment. Military records contain health, education, employment, and psychological information. Any military security clearance also includes arrest records, FBI information, fingerprints, prior addresses, and, frequently, unsubstantiated statements made by prior neighbors, employers, and acquaintances. Credit bureaus share information from most credit card and consumer credit issuers. This information is shared openly with minimal restrictions. Another frequently requested piece of information is an employment history and references. A prior employer may have information on lie detector tests, drug tests, and intelligence test scores, as well as unsubstantiated allegations by disgruntled coworkers or supervisors.

But the argument in favor of public disclosure of individual information is just as compelling. The restricted use of available information is costly. Tax records are valuable to any type of criminal prosecution that involves the movement of money. This includes bribery, extortion, embezzlement, theft, gambling, or selling illegal drugs, stolen property, or pornography. The ethical issue is really more than a simple question of privacy versus public disclosure. There is an obvious need for truly personal information to be protected from the curious and malicious. There is an equally compelling need to collect and maintain personal information to administer public programs. But the cost of creating duplicate files for each separate program is enormous. The trade-off between privacy rights and cost-effective service delivery forces a choice between greater privacy and higher costs, and less privacy and lower costs.

POLITICAL GAMES VERSUS MANAGERIAL EXCELLENCE

When administrative ethics are intertwined with political strategies, the ethical dilemmas become incredibly complex and difficult to separate. The next case demonstrates how frustrating it is to be a midlevel manager in a federal agency with no control over the decision to shut down the agency for a day during a congressional budget brouhaha.

Case: Shutting Federal Offices

The federal agency for which Dennis Walbank worked was shut down at 1:00 P.M. on October 4, 1984, for two reasons. First, Congress and the Reagan administration had failed to agree on a budget to cover this and most other federal agencies. Second, the Democrats and Republicans in Congress were unable to agree on some alternative solution to agency funding, such as a continuing resolution to authorize unbudgeted spending. Under the Reagan administration this was the second time such action had been ordered, the first being November 23, 1981. As a result, agencies had developed the procedures to shut down operations quickly and without confusion.

Walbank was notified by his regional office of the impending halt to operations at about 11:00 A.M. He discussed the procedures with the division chief and carried out the familiar procedure. He was allowed to retain one essential person at each major office statewide, along with two in the agency's state headquarters office. This amounted to seven persons from a work force of approximately one hundred fifty around the entire state. The seven who remained simply stopped service to the public and caught up on administrative tasks until the continuing resolution was passed overnight and personnel were called back to work the next day.

Ethical Issues

The values involved in this are *accountability*, *pursuit of excellence*, and *promise keeping* in the case of elected officials who ran for office promising more effective government and less waste. From the perspective of the public employee, *loyalty* to an order by the president of the United States is at stake. *Responsible citizenship* is also included in terms of elected officials' and public employees' obligations to promote the public interest.

Alternatives

Congress could reform its processes and provide a timely, meaningful financial structure for government. The current process is a cannibalistic one where the president, in effect, eats away at parts of his own tribe, the executive branch, in order to posture for members of another tribe, the Congress. The taxpayer becomes both spectator and victim.

Resolution

The closure was obviously inefficient in terms of lost workdays. Not only did the government lose the time while the employees were furloughed, but the appropriations bill contained the funds to pay the furloughed employees, who received an unplanned, paid vacation as a result. In addition, the planning, administration, and postfurlough actions added to the costs. No money is every saved from such political theater, and productivity is hampered.

WHISTLE-BLOWING

It is not possible to talk about responsible citizenship for long without talking about whistle-blowing. "Whistleblowing is the act of a man or woman who believes that the public interest overrides the interest of the organization he or she serves" (Mathews, 1987, p. 40). It is going public with information regarding product safety, aiming to spotlight neglect or abuse of the public interest, or spotlighting procedures that run counter to company policy or public expectations.

Whistle-blowing is analogous to civil disobedience. Frederick Elliston (1982) compares the two forms of dissent: civil disobedience is protests by citizens against the laws or actions of their government, and whistle-blowing is disclosure by employees of illegal, immoral, or questionable practices by their employer or fellow employees. Civil disobedience is defined by three criteria: (1) the action must be illegal, (2) the action must be done for a moral reason, and (3) the action must be done in order to change a law that is found objectionable (Elliston, 1982). Furthermore, the person who engages in civil disobedience must be respectful of the rule of law by accepting the punishment for the crime committed by the disobedience. The rules of a business are usually followed by its employees, as are the laws of governments. When a company's rules are broken for moral reasons, it is called whistle-blowing. When citizens break government rules, it is called civil disobedience.

Many people believe that civil disobedience should be undertaken as a last resort. They argue that letters to elected representatives, petitions to city hall, grassroots organizing, and other active lobbying efforts should take place before resorting to disobedience. Similar beliefs surround whistle-blowing. Many people believe that the whistle-blower should exhaust all internal channels before bringing in outside factors. However, this approach takes precious time that may delay the immediate response that may be needed.

Whistle-blowers usually belong to and feel an allegiance with the organization they report. If they feel little allegiance they are more likely either not to care about the problem enough to blow the whistle or to leave the firm altogether. The fact that they are ego-invested in the company makes the act of blowing the whistle more difficult because it means that if they do so, they will forfeit the goodwill they enjoy on the job. The whistle-blower must reconcile conflict between loyalty to the employer and loyalty to the public. A whistle-blower must choose among "goods." Allegations of misconduct have to be made only on the basis of substantial evidence. Such allegations are a very serious matter, and the parties involved must take measures to assure that the rights and reputations of all individuals named in such allegations and all individuals who in good faith report apparent misconduct are protected. When internal systems are ineffective, however, a whistle-blower must go outside the company to the public. But this behavior is considered insubordinate, and the person will be accused of violating confidentiality and of being disloyal to the company. Employers do not want employees to go to outside authorities with a complaint. When this happens, they lose control over the situation and, if the information is *not* correct, it causes needless embarrassment to the company.

Most people come forward when their accusations are well founded, are very serious, and involve large sums of money or danger to the public. "Most employees do not see it as their role to report wrongdoing unless it is particularly egregious" (Near, 1989, p. 3). These people are normal employees who have tipped the balance of their loyalty toward the public good rather than toward the organization for which they work.

Blowing the whistle anonymously is an option that is open to employees but is discouraged. Anonymous whistle-blowing lies somewhere between secrecy and privacy. The primary justification for anonymity is the seriousness of the offense and the probability of unfair retaliation.

When dissent is solely internal or is anonymous, the person reporting the immoral actions has some degree of power over the situation, while taking less personal risk. However, when whistle-blowers do not go public with complaints, they cannot participate in the actual debate to present their side and defend it.

In reality, most employees keep their feet firmly planted in expediency and choose to fight only the battles that are essential. In the face of serious dissent, they have the choice of resigning, disagreeing openly, or being silent. But the choice of exit, voice, or loyalty only touches the surface of the complex results of dissent. The open airing of internal differences can genuinely weaken organizational morale and reduce the capacity to accomplish objectives (Fleishman and Payne, 1980).

Frequently, the person who has the courage to blow the whistle is fired or harassed. Much corporate crime continues because of people's willingness to look the other way when wrongdoing occurs. They know that they may get into trouble for reporting it. When whistle-blowers decide to "tattle" on a peer, they risk their careers and reputations to benefit unknown and unknowing strangers. When someone tattled as a child, everyone got in trouble. This carries into adulthood, and when an employee blows the whistle, many people are hurt.

Should I tell on this person or not? At first glance, this seems to be a fairly simple question. To be phrased more accurately, the question should ask: Should I risk my career and get my boss or coworkers fired in order to solve a problem? Should I ignore the chain of command and go to higher authorities with the problem? If I am a wrong, what will happen to me? How will everyone think of me after this? Will the higher authorities think the same as the person on whom I am blowing the whistle? On whose side will they be? Will the ends justify the means? The question of whether or not to report wrongdoing becomes very complex very quickly.

Some protection against retaliation is available to whistle-blowers, but they must prove that they were fired or demoted directly because of the whistle-blowing act. This is often difficult to prove, especially since the employer can say that the employee was fired for other reasons. Although some states have banned retaliatory firings, other state courts upheld rulings that employees have been unjustly fired but have awarded no damages (Sheler, 1981). Still other states have ruled that employers have a right to fire at will unless barred by union contract. The Whistleblower Protection Act of 1989 assures confidentiality to federal employees who report wrongdoing and gives them the right to appeal a retaliatory action on the part of the employer (McCormick, 1989).

Ebasco Constructors Inc., a company that owns a nuclear plant, was accused of discrimination by an employee who was fired in April 1986 (*ENR*, 1988). An employee, Ronald J. Goldstein, had reported safety and quality-control violations. In the summer of 1985, Goldstein complained that the company had failed to follow required construction sequences, alterations, and inspection procedures for pipe installation. When uncovered, these mistakes were explained by Ebasco engineers as "important," but not "earthshattering." The judge in Goldstein's case ruled that although Goldstein was seen as disruptive and complaining at the company, his complaints about these safety violations were correct. Since he took his concerns to outside authorities, the judge suggested that Goldstein was fired as a retaliatory measure. The firing was considered discrimination (*ENR*, 1988).

Lawrence Archer (1986) cites a study that suggests that out of every ten whistle-blowers, only one is still employed with the firm that employed them when they blew the whistle. Individuals who had filed complaints of unfair employment discrimination completed questionnaires about the retaliation that followed their whistle-blowing. Analyses revealed that organizations were more likely to retaliate against whistle-blowers who were valued by the organization because of their age, experience, or education and against whistle-blowers whose cases lacked public support than against other whistle-blowers (Parmerlee, Near, and Jansen, 1982). Retribution does not seem to curb the behavior of determined whistle-blowers. In fact, Janet Near's research (1989) shows that those who have been retaliated against are more likely to blow the whistle again than those who are not retaliated against.

Retaliation by the employer depends on the company's perception of the correctness of the whistle-blowing regarding both the facts and the right of the whistle-blower to make the complaint. Marcia Parmerlee, Janet Near, and Tamila Jansen (1982) found the following company responses:

- If the company feels the complaint is legitimate and the employee has a right to express his complaint, they will usually resolve it internally.
- The company may cooperate with an outside investigative agency to correct their wrongs but act toward the employee as if no complaint had been filed.

- The company may decide to "agree" with the complaint and settle the matter quickly and quietly to avoid bad publicity.

- The company may resolve the problem at lower levels, not even bringing upper management into the matter.

- The company may completely block outside interference and discourage the complaint and future complaints.

- The company may use legal pressure to get whistle-blowers to drop a complaint or they may resort to isolating them, defaming their character, excluding them from important meetings, and impugning their motives.

Moral conflict exists when persons recognize that their inclination to blow the whistle might lead to a violation of fundamental norms that their friends hold. From those who object to whistle-blowing, it is often considered a violation of comradeship and confidence. For example, the informal norm of professionals requires collegial loyalty, while professional groups' codes of ethics usually stress responsibility to the public over and above duties to colleagues and clients (Dozier and Miceli, 1985). The Association of Professional Engineers of Ontario (APEO) is a professional organization that punishes members who do not practice their professional code of ethics. However, the very same members face disciplinary action from the company they work for if they *do* find a dangerous situation and practice their professional code of ethics by blowing the whistle (Archer, 1986).

Whistle-blowers risk quite a bit when they decide to go forward with their accusations of wrongdoing: careers, friends, reputations, as well as employability in their chosen field. If a whistle-blower files a grievance regarding harassment, all his or her shortcomings as an employee will be brought up. Several nationally recognized people have blown the whistle over the years and encountered various responses:

- Karen Silkwood filed a complaint that her employer, the Kerr-McGee nuclear plant, was mishandling plutonium and needlessly exposing workers to radioactivity. She suffered a mysterious death that was never fully explained (McGowan, 1985).

- Frank Serpico reported corruption in New York City and was later killed during a raid. There is still some doubt as to whether his partners had anything to do with his death (McGowan, 1985).

- Rick Parks reported that Bechtel, a nuclear management company, was not conducting quality-control tests and was taking many safety shortcuts. He was harassed on the job and was later transferred, suspended, and then laid off. His charges against Bechtel were finally verified in May 1984.

- A. Ernest Fitzgerald was a cost analyst for the Defense Department in 1969 when he reported the Air Force for cost overruns. He was fired, but in 1982, after a long legal battle, he was given back his original job.

- Bill Bush reported NASA's Marshall Space Flight Center for reassigning older engineers to menial, unfamiliar jobs to force their early retirement. Bush was ostracized when he filed charges with the Civil Service Commission. He retains a position with NASA but is treated as if he were a pariah by many of his peers.

- An ex-employee of the Department of Defense, George Spanton, spoke out about wrongdoing he discovered in 1981 (Miller, 1985). He had found illegal billings from a Defense Department contractor based in West Palm Beach. When the Defense Department did not act on Spanton's discovery, he went public with the information. Because he did so, his boss tried to transfer him long before his scheduled rotation. His transfer was eventually blocked, and he was allowed to remain in West Palm Beach, where he retired in 1983.

The list does not stop. When Dr. Grace Pierce refused to continue work on a drug that contained large amounts of saccharin (a suspected carcinogen), she was demoted and not considered for any more senior assignments (Chalk, 1988). She resigned from Ortho Pharmaceuticals and sued the company for wrongful discharge. The New Jersey Supreme Court acknowledged that she had acted according to her conscience, but since she had failed to point out any legislation on which her decision was made, the court did not rule in her favor.

Ethical Aspects of Whistle-Blowing

Many managers face difficult decisions about their own ethical conduct as well as that of their employees. For example, if a coworker makes a habit of taking pens and paper home for her children, does the manager have a responsibility to report it? Should she risk pointing her finger at another colleague? One suggestion to reduce possible career risk from whistle-blowing is to talk to the employee directly, instead of to his or her supervisor (Byrne, 1987). Merely warning the employee that someone knows about the questionable behavior may warrant a change. If the employee is not in good standing anyway, there is less risk involved in blowing the whistle. However, if the employee is in good standing and has exemplary performance, the company may decide to overlook the wrongdoing.

Revealing information becomes ethical when it will save someone from being hurt or mistreated or when it will keep someone's rights from being violated. In some cases it would even be unethical for someone *not* to blow the whistle. A deciding factor is whether or not the ratio of "good" to "evil" warrants the whistle-blowing. The "evil" represents the breaking of confidence when whistle-blowers reveal their information. In any situation in which the question of whether or not someone should blow the whistle arises, the end should justify the means. The following case presents a typical whistle-blowing scenario.

Case: Flawed Construction

Sally Seymour (1988) poses this scenario: when a fifteen-year-old report of flawed construction of a nuclear reactor was found by a lower-level employee at Fairway Electric, he brought the matter to the attention of the vice president of the nuclear division. The report had been drawn up by engineers in 1973 and was found accidentally when the employee's secretary was cleaning out some old files. It stated that the engineers had found the flaw and reported it to their supervisors then. However, a memorandum had been circulated that said that the flaw was not a safety problem and the costs of reconstruction would be disastrous for the company. Nothing was done to correct the problem, and it was then brushed under the carpet. Fifteen years later, when the employee reported the problem to the vice president, the vice president then reported it to the CEO, who told him to forget it and tell the employee to forget it, too. When pressed on the matter, the CEO stated that the problem was not one of safety and that if the flaw was made public now, it would cost the company a great deal. He said to bury it! The vice president then went back to the employee and told him the same thing. The employee was irate, and began to lose respect for the company. He researched the plant where the flawed design had been constructed and found that the utility company had paid large sums to have the flaw repaired several years after the construction had been completed. The company had passed on the expense of repairing the flaw to the ratepayers. He felt the public should know the costs that they had inevitably paid due to increased utility bills. Since internal channels of communication had not worked, the employee went to the newspapers.

When the story came out, Fairway made no comment. The pressure from demonstrators, press, and politicians soon became so great that management decided to make a statement and come clean. Although the public controversy eventually died down, pressures inside the company did not. Coworkers no longer trusted the employee who had reported the story. They did not want to work with him anymore, and their production rate went down markedly. When the CEO heard of this, he asked the vice president to talk with the employee and "influence" him to "voluntarily" quit. The vice president tried instead to get the employee to transfer because he believed that he was a talented individual and the company needed him. The employee balked, and the vice president then began to question what he should have done.

Ethical Issues

Honesty was clearly involved in this case, on the part of the company, as was *accountability*. The *integrity* of the employee was at stake and he felt a compelling role as a responsible citizen. The employee expected the company to put the *pursuit of excellence* above monetary concerns and was flabbergasted when they did not. He believed the information should be made public because he knew a public outcry would cause the company to make reparations.

Alternatives

The vice president could have begun an effort in his department to encourage employees to come forward with concerns and had a constructive procedure for handling concerns as soon as they became known.

The vice president could have supported the employee who reported the discovered flaw. Initially, he should have agreed on an effective plan of action in dealing with the situation. Alternative channels of communication should also have been open to the whistle-blower, so he could go to someone else besides the newspapers when his vice president and CEO did not support him.

Resolution

If the vice president supported the employee, he would be sending a message that he supported honesty in the company as well as the fact that he supported the integrity of the employee who brought the problem to light. If he insisted on transferring the employee, he would be sending a message that any whistle-blowers, no matter how correct their complaints, would be treated punitively.

If a company seems to condone wrongdoing, potential whistle-blowers have to examine their personal codes of ethics and compare them to the perceived ethics of the company. If they do not match and there is a large gap in between, perhaps they should consider a job change.

The question of whether or not to blow the whistle is not reserved to those who work in large anonymous bureaucracies. The following case typifies the predicament of an employee working in a small art gallery. As she became aware that the accounts were being kept dishonestly, she had to decide whether or not to take action.

Case: The Art Gallery

When Rita Barlow accepted a part-time job at a small art gallery and framery, her responsibilities included sales and generally being a flunky. She soon discovered that art sales were a natural for her. She enjoyed the combination of craft and people skills. Soon she was selling more in twenty hours per week than anyone else was selling in forty hours.

After Barlow had been there about three months, the owner-in-residence (there were two silent partners) asked her to become manager. It seemed like fun, and she agreed. They discussed a small raise plus a percentage of sales increases as commission. It was a small business with only four full-time employees other than Barlow, three part-timers who worked during busy seasons, and several free-lancers who received discounted materials and did their own labor. At first it seemed that all was well. In the twenty or so months that Barlow was manager, sales tripled. She expanded the market to include commercial sales, coordinated shows with local artists, did residential consultation, and conducted seminars. All this was done without an increase in staff.

Barlow was having too much fun to fret over not receiving the promised commission and receiving only minimal increases in salary. She enjoyed all aspects of the business: ordering materials, being abreast of the local art community, working with businesses and individuals, and managing the personnel and work flow. The owner dropped by now and then to pay the bills. Other than that, she had control.

Gradually she began to notice that the shop was getting what seemed to be statements from accounts that should have been paid long before. Occasionally supplies would arrive with a "payment on delivery" demand. A favorite supplier mysteriously stopped calling. Artists with whom the store had a good working relationship suddenly became very cool and stopped coming in. Nevertheless, the volume of business continued to grow due to new sources.

It all came to a climax when Barlow's bank notified her that her paycheck had bounced. The store's accounting was done by an outside firm, but she had access to all the records. That same evening after work, she was able to figure that the store should have been making somewhere in the range of 250 percent profit. When the owner came by a couple of days later, Barlow showed him the returned check and related what the bank had said. He mumbled something about the accountant and wrote another check on another account.

Barlow concluded that money was being diverted from the business. And she had a fairly good idea that it was being done without the knowledge of the partners. She was confronted with several possible scenarios, all unpleasant. Should she confront the owner with her charges, asking for explanations? Should she confide her suspicions to the partners? Should she continue to seek out new customers and suppliers when she did not have assurance that they would be treated fairly? Should she continue to gloss over the problems with the employees? Should she pretend that nothing was wrong? Should she resign?

Ethical Issues

In this case, the harm that was being done was to employees who were not receiving their paychecks on time and suppliers who were not being paid. Barlow *cared* about their welfare and worried about what would happen to those around her as a result of the outcome of this dilemma. Barlow wanted to respond *honestly* when asked by suppliers and peers why checks were not forthcoming. As a manager at the shop, she was *accountable* to those who had a stake in the enterprise. She wanted to be involved in the *pursuit of excellence*, not in a cover-up operation. She wanted to remain *loyal* to the employees, the partners, the suppliers, and the customers. However, she found herself in a dilemma where she had to decide where her greatest loyalty lay. And she wanted to protect her *integrity* and not be involved in a shady operation.

Alternatives

Barlow was confronted with these choices: to leave the shop, to speak up about her concerns, or to continue at the shop but say nothing to anyone about its bookkeeping practices. In other words, she was faced with the classic choice of exit, voice, or loyalty. To leave meant she would preserve her integrity but disregard the need she felt to be honest about what was going on. Furthermore, it would minimize loyalty and caring. To stay and do nothing would run the risk of her being viewed, in the long run, as guilty by association. And her inaction would minimize honesty, accountability, pursuit of excellence, and integrity. To stay and give voice to her concerns would contribute to caring, honesty, accountability, pursuing excellence, and integrity, but she stood the risk of being labeled as a troublemaker and fired.

Resolution

After a few days of doing nothing, she concluded that she was in a no-win situation. After a while, she made the owner aware of what she knew. She began to work fewer hours and began to withdraw emotionally from the job. When she talked with the partners, it was obvious that they were unaware of what was happening. Within three months, she resigned. The end of the story for the business came when one morning the sheriff's department came and took everything away.

There is not much evidence to show why some employees report wrongdoing and others do not. Marcia Miceli and Janet Near (1984) tested whether individuals' positions and their beliefs and perceptions regarding organizational conditions would differentiate personnel of three types. Respondents employed by fifteen federal agencies responded to a mailed questionnaire. Of thirteen thousand randomly selected subjects who received questionnaires, 68 percent responded. Three types of employees were examined in this study: those who had not observed wrongdoing, those who had observed it but did not report it, and those who had observed it and had blown the whistle (Miceli and Near, 1984). The results showed that:

a. Actual whistle-blowers welcome the act more than people who do not blow the whistle, and also believe that the employer should encourage it.

b. People who do not observe wrongdoing say they are more likely than those who do observe it to blow the whistle for incentives such as seeing action taken, but are less likely to do it for cash incentives.

c. Whistle-blowers know available complaint channels better than those who do not blow the whistle.

d. People who are better educated and have higher salaries, and are therefore more independent of the company, are quicker to blow the whistle than are others, probably because they are in less jeopardy of threatening their livelihood.

e. Employees who blow the whistle inside the organization more often hold higher positions than whistle-blowers who go to the press.

f. Whistle-blowers who use external means for reporting wrongdoing, such as the press, have higher pay levels than internal whistle-blowers but less education. Also, they do not rely on incentives to blow the whistle, think they have more knowledge of how to report wrongdoing, and are more approving of whistle-blowing than other employees.

g. Those who observe wrongdoing but do not report it tend to be lower paid, highly educated "fast trackers" who probably fear their career aspirations will be on the line if they blow the whistle.

The final conclusion of the study was that finding the right encouragements or inducements for whistle-blowers is a problem. Employees have been socialized to avoid organizational dissidence. To convince them otherwise, that authority structures permit whistle-blowing, is difficult.

SUMMARY

Good citizenship is not the preserve of any one segment of the population. It is a challenge to everyone: large corporations and small businesses, individual employees at all levels of employment, and communities as a whole. Ethical questions that involve the issue of citizenship arise in a variety of circumstances, including when to protect versus when to share confidential information, weighing the good to the community against the good to the individual, and blowing the whistle on wrongdoing.

The cases in this chapter demonstrate the frustrations and complexity that come with accepting one's responsibility to look out for the welfare of others. Paying one's civic rent is necessary and sometimes very expensive. But ethical business behavior encourages trust between business professionals, between employees within a company, and between companies and their clients, and it is the basis of successful relationships between people (Smith, 1986).

Open, available internal channels within organizations encourage employees to voice their concerns and objections without fear of recrimination or retaliation. It is to the employer's benefit to remedy problems early, thereby preserving employees' trust as well as the company's reputation. Trust is essential between employer and employee. If employees trust employers to resolve concerns through internal means, they are less likely to go to external channels to report wrongdoing (Mathews, 1987). Protecting whistleblowers sends the message that the organization expects and is responsive to individual morality in the corporate structure (Hauserman, 1986). In fact, fair treatment of whistle-blowers may be the most dramatic way to persuade employees to operate ethically.

When ethical considerations are brought into the policies and procedures of companies, people find it commonplace to practice ethical conduct. Such an atmosphere establishes an ethical reputation for the company and the individuals it employs.

7

Guidelines for Ethical Decision Making

Ethics is about how we treat each other, every day, person to person. If you want to know about a company's ethics, look at how it treats people—customers, suppliers and employees. Business is about people. And business ethics is about how customers and employees are treated.

—R. Edward Freeman

Ethical responsibility is personal responsibility. A group cannot act ethically until its members, as individuals, choose to do so. When individuals act ethically, together they produce a group action that is ethical.

CHAPELFIRZ

Values shape the way problems are perceived. They are crucial to our notion that something is a problem to be solved rather than accepted. And the values of those who actively implement decisions affect the actual shape of the ultimate policy. By the time a decision maker has taken caring, honesty, accountability, promise keeping, pursuit of excellence, loyalty, fairness, integrity, respect for others, and responsible citizenship into consideration, that person can be assured that a thorough analysis of ethical values has been made. Each value adds a dimension to the analysis. While some are redundant over others or add little, taking each into consideration ensures that the decision maker is sensitive to all possible ethical dimensions of the problem.

ETHICAL DECISION MAKING

When ethical analysis is blended with decision making, ethical decisions result. In order to reach an ethical decision, one must define the problem and determine the desired end result. The values to be maximized must be identified, and all aspects of the problem must be analyzed to see which values are involved. After this, alternatives to each dimension of the problem have to be identified and assessed to learn which values will be maximized and which will be minimized. Ultimately, the alternative which does the best job of maximizing the most important values while still resolving the problem is the desirable choice.

In reality, choices are rarely made directly between values. Rather, they are made between options that differ in the extent to which they embody particular values or in the emphasis some values receive in relation to others. Ethical decisions are decisions that result from a reasoned choice among goods, and only rarely from a choice between good and evil.

ETHICAL SATISFICING

People make the best decision they can, given the constraints of the situation. Decision making in work situations is a complex task because of the number of influences that affect the decision calculus. The problem itself presents the central issue, but consideration is moderated by a number of factors, including the wishes of those who are affected by the problem, the opportunities and costs associated with solving the problem, the knowledge and interests of the person who ultimately makes the decision, and the likelihood of being able to implement the decision as it is intended.

Most problems involve two or more values, and a comparison between them is inevitable, such that a greater return to one can be obtained only at a loss to the other. Not everything is known about the situation, and anticipated consequences cannot be predicted with certainty. And the power to make the decision is dispersed over a multitude of people and/or departments. Because of their proclivity to satisfice, people will seek rules of thumb regarding which values are most important. Ideally,

Figure 7.1
Ethical Decision Making

the decision maker will determine the fundamental values to be maximized and then weigh the probable impact of each alternative. In reality, only the most obvious values are analyzed and a full consideration of all dimensions of the problem will not occur. This is why it is incumbent upon organizations to clearly communicate those values that are most important. Even if other values are not considered, at least the most important ones will be considered during the problem-solving process. Figure 7.1 illustrates the array of values that influence a problem and affect ethical decision making.

Ethical decision making is the process of identifying a problem, generating alternatives, and choosing among them so that the alternatives selected maximize the most important ethical values while also achieving the intended goal. Not all values can be maximized simultaneously. Some must be compromised in order for others to be maximized. This compromise is ethical satisficing.

Most work-related decisions have an ethical component. With few exceptions, problems that involve people also involve ethical issues. Decisions that affect people's jobs and careers have an ethical component. Decisions that involve conflicts of commitment or obligation have an ethical component. Decisions that involve how people should behave on the job have an ethical component. And decisions that involve basic freedoms and civic responsibilities have an ethical component. Only the simplest, most mechanical of decisions are spared ethical analysis.

Assessing Long-Term and Short-Term Effects of Decisions

The time dimension complicates already complicated problems. What may appear to be an ethical decision at the present time may prove unethical in the future. What may prove to be the right thing to do in the distant future may seem unreasoned at the present. Reviewing some of the cases in the previous chapters shows why. For example, the fact that Trumplit had been accepting gift certificates from a building owner for years but not cashing them in seemed appropriate while he was an office manager. However, when he was promoted into a position where he was in charge of arranging office rental space for offices around the state, it was apparent that his decision years earlier would ruin his credibility if it were to become public knowledge.

On the other hand, the decision by Donohue not to accept gifts from his Korean counterparts seemed quarrelsome in the short term. His colleagues did not understand why he made such a fuss over a commonly accepted practice. However, in the long run, it paved the way for those who succeeded him to practice the same policy and avoid compromising their judgment.

Bledsoe's decision not to print the political flyer seemed shortsighted in the short run but paid off in the long run. Her integrity was respected, she received promotions, she respected her supervisor, and he respected her. In fact, they mutually admired one another's integrity. Had she agreed to print the flyer and done so against her beliefs, she would have grown to resent the supervisor, and the supervisor would have assumed that Bledsoe did not mind printing such jobs and would be willing to do more of the same. Had Bledsoe agreed to the first printing and then refused to do a subsequent printing of a similar job, she would have had to explain that not only did she not appreciate being asked to do the job, she had not wanted to do the first job either. Trust would have diminished within the relationship.

When Captain Johnson was asked to assume a position as personnel officer, he solved the short-range problem that the battalion commander was facing. However, in the long run the battalion commander's request caused Johnson to forfeit a position that would have led to further promotions in his chosen career. Johnson's loyalty was never compensated and his career changed drastically because of it. Examples could go on and on. Suffice it to say that for a decision to be ethical, it must account not only for short-term consequences, but also for long-term effects.

CREATING AN ETHICAL CULTURE

Actions speak louder than words. Leaders in all organizations must understand that in order to be ethical and promote ethics, they must go beyond the mere letter of the law as stated in their companies' codes of ethics. Merely observing a rule does not necessarily make one's behavior ethical. A failure to affirm basic ethical norms conveys a message that values are of little concern or importance in that organization.

The values that are shared by most of the organization's members mark the foundation of the culture. When these values promote CHAPELFIRZ, the foundation is laid for an ethical culture. Just as values serve as a guide to a person's intentions and actions, an organization's values provide guides for organizational goals, policies, and strategies. The operational values of an organization are those that guide members' decisions on day-to-day matters. To be functional, these values concern the mode of conduct of members and focus on goals, functions, and operational procedures. They deal with issues of product quality, customer satisfaction, and innovation (Wiener, 1988). Socialization to these values is an essential process that precedes the institutionalization of an ethical culture. As new members join the organization, the culture is perpetuated in the indoctrination process. Those who violate the acceptable norms of the culture are sanctioned in such a way that it sends a message to everyone else about which behaviors will not be tolerated. Ethical organizations are not created as much by enforcement as they are by peer pressure. Personnel will be reluctant to engage in activities that are frowned upon by those whom they respect. Enforcement efforts following a breach of ethics are not as effective as proactively training employees to make ethical decisions.

Establishing such ethical norms in an organization has to start from the beginning with new employees because prior to employment, personnel may not have been expected to be sensitive to the ethical components of problems. Students pass through the public-school and college systems watching their peers cheat on homework. In 1987, 56 percent of college freshmen surveyed across the nation reported that they had copied homework during their high school years, and 32 percent acknowledged that they had cheated on a test (Zumberge, 1989). Many employers are discouraged with how insensitive workers are to the ethical dimensions of problems. Allan Bloom (1987) castigates the parents of today for having produced a generation without the moral background to evaluate problems. He thinks the American family's moral training comes down to inculcating the bare minima of social appropriateness, that is, not lying or stealing, and produces young adults who can say nothing more about the basis of their moral trespasses than "If I did that to him, he could do it to me" (Bloom, 1987, p. 61).

Simply abiding by the law does not ensure ethical behavior. Laws merely set minimum standards for legally acceptable behavior in areas that have been tested and agreed upon by legislatures. Many behaviors are not covered by the law but are clearly unethical. In fact, ethics almost always calls for greater diligence than that required by law in protecting the rights of others (Sanderson and Varner, 1984). For example, in February 1989 a retired air force colonel, Robert L. Hedges, was convicted on a conflict-of-interest charge for having negotiated a postretirement consulting contract with the Sperry Corporation while still on active duty and supervising the air force's $526-million computer contract with Sperry. Hedges's defense, with which the jury did not agree, was that he had followed the letter of the law. He claimed that he had cleared the consulting contract with an air force lawyer, had notified his superior officer that Sperry had contacted him about the job, and contended that he had taken every step required by air force regulations to avoid a conflict of interest. But following the letter of law is not the same as making decisions on the ethics of the matter. In this case, as in many cases, what was clearly a breach of ethics was still within the letter of the law (*Birmingham Post-Herald*, 1989). In response to the jury's conviction, the prosecutor was quoted as saying, "This puts vitality and meaning into the conflict-of-interest statutes" (p. A10).

While a violation of the law is associated with a fine or other penalty, a violation of ethics is more likely to be associated with a troubled conscience, dissatisfaction at work, and perhaps a loss of self-respect. It is not unusual for this to deteriorate into an inability to trust others. Since people tend to treat their own behavior as the lowest common denominator of everyone's behavior, everyone else is held to the standard one holds for oneself. When someone knows that his or her own behavior has breached ethical parameters, that person is likely to assume that others do also. This cripples trust. For example, if personnel are accustomed to padding their expense vouchers, they will assume that "everyone else does it, why shouldn't I?" In fact, their assumption may be only their projection of their own behavior onto others. The more individuals there are who are sensitive to ethical considerations, the more influence their sensitivity will have on their ethical decisions, and the more newcomers to the organization will develop their own sensitivity. In fact, O. C. Ferrell and Larry Gresham (1985) argue that unethical behavior is influenced by the ratio of contacts with unethical patterns to contacts with ethical patterns.

The word *sensitivity* keeps being used because there are no hard and fast rules that apply to all circumstances, without some breaches being punished by draconian penalties. Most people agree that stealing is wrong. But the consensus lessens as the value of the gain and the circumstances surrounding the intent of the stealing move from embezzling company funds to padding an expense voucher to pilfering pencils and erasers and poster board from a company's supply cabinet for a child's homework project.

Ethical business practices stem from an ethical corporate culture. The challenge is to create and nourish the culture so that ethical considerations of issues are routinely made before decisions are made. More and more, business schools are facing the fact that ethical decision making should be an integral part of the training for tomorrow's managers (Magner, 1989). A national survey of professors who teach administrative ethics to public administration students showed that the most important factor in ethical decision making is the ability to assess the moral principles and probable consequences in ethical dilemmas (Hejka-Ekins, 1988).

Corporate Codes of Conduct

Corporate codes of ethics are important because they provide visible guidelines. Codes offer a touchstone for guidance and remind every employee to look beyond simple expediency. A study of codes of ethics concluded that there are only three broad clusters of topics in most codes (Robin et al., 1989). These three relate to being a dependable citizen of the organization, refraining from any action that would be unlawful or improper, and being good to customers and clients. For example, the code of ethics for certified computer professionals emphasizes obligations to the public at large to be knowledgeable of their field, to the profession to uphold high ideals and disseminate knowledge pertaining to the development of the profession, and to their employers to serve their interests and the interests of the employers' clients (Association of the ICCP, 1988). The code for certified public accountants stresses integrity, objectivity, independent judgment, and responsibility to the public interest. In fact, the American Institute of Certified Public Accountants runs advertisements in national newsmagazines promoting the ethical standards of their members (American Institute of Certified Public Accountants, 1989).

In 1984 Glen Sanderson and Iris Varner collected thirty-nine codes of conduct from the top one hundred Fortune 500 corporations. They analyzed these codes for their content, purpose, and organization. After studying all of them, they realized that the codes included only nine major topics. And there was no major difference in the topics covered relating to the industry in which the corporation was engaged. The nine topics are

- conflicts of interest
- political contributions
- relations with customers and suppliers
- accurate record keeping
- antitrust matters
- equal employment
- product safety and environmental responsibility
- protecting confidential information
- theft by employees

About three-fourths of the content of these codes related to complying with federal laws and referred their readers to their corporate legal departments for more information. This is the easiest way out for a corporate code of conduct, since it does not rely on individual analysis of conduct. It is also the least effective at promoting an ethical culture. Many activities are within the law but outside the parameters of ethical behavior.

While codes may communicate specific rules, they have little impact on the immediate problems that crop up in daily organizational activities and operations. In other words, they offer no specific guidance on how to make values-based decisions. Instead, they serve as rough guidelines. Some organizations strengthen their codes with implementation guidelines and enforcement procedures, but this is the exception rather than the rule. In summary, codes of ethics are helpful, but they stop far short of ensuring ethical decision making.

A systematic approach to building and nurturing structures that emphasize the importance of ethical considerations is important. Corporate credos, training programs, and codes of ethics that are clearly understood by employees provide such structures (Murphy, 1989). Credos are succinct statements of the values permeating the firm. They work best in firms with a cohesive culture, where a spirit of frequent and open communication exists (Murphy, 1989). Credos set forth good general principles, but they must be operationalized into terms employees at all levels of the organization understand before they are meaningful. Much like the trailer signs parked in front of churches that admonish passersby to live their lives on the "straight and narrow," constant repetition is necessary to remind everyone. Training programs are useful when they are tailored to discussions of situations that participants recognize and confront often. In order to train people to be sensitive throughout their workday, they must be able to translate their workshop experience directly into their own jobs. As Patrick Murphy (1989) warns, "If the credo can be compared with the Ten Commandments, then ethics programs can be likened to weekly church services. Both can be uplifting, but once the session (service) is over, individuals may believe they can go back to business as usual" (p. 85). Codes of ethics are necessary in large firms where the work force is widely distributed. In small firms where the work force see one another daily and where a culture includes firmly entrenched, meaningful ethical policies, they are redundant. They will do no harm, but they may fail to enhance what is already in motion.

Truly ethical behavior requires that one go beyond the bare minimum and act responsibly, with due regard for the well-being of society, the organization, and all its stakeholders. Despite codes of ethics and ethical cultures, organizations do not make decisions. Codes of ethics help, but control lies within each individual. Individuals make the decisions. The greater one's integrity, the greater one's ability to carefully analyze a situation and make an ethical decision. A respect for self and others, a willingness to sacrifice for the common good, a sense of civic responsibility, the relentless pursuit of truth, basic honesty, and an intolerance for anything less is a measure of the character of a person (Roskens, 1988; Wade, 1988).

Hot lines within companies, codes of ethics, and corrupt-practices laws attempt to prevent ethical dilemmas from occurring. But these cannot supplant ethical decision making. They can only supplement what is within the individual, which is his or her own set of principles applied to discrete decisions. The best position executives can be in is one that promotes ethical behavior in their organizations, rather than one that results in the predicament of having to put out fires caused by someone's failure to realize the ethical dimension of a problem.

STRATEGIC ETHICAL RESPONSE

There is a commonality of ethical concerns across all management functions, including planning, organizing, staffing, directing, coordinating, reporting, and budgeting. It is naive to assume that ethical sensitivity is only relevant at certain levels in an organization or is the province of certain departments, such as the legal department.

The crucial task for all personnel is to identify the ethical issues in the midst of all the complexity and moral uncertainty of the contexts of the situation. Moral reasoning is fundamentally about the conscious choices of individuals in relation to actions affecting others. Many of the loyalties, interests, and preconceptions that actually shape policy preferences or determine an organization's agenda are at best only partly conscious in the minds of those who make decisions (Fleishman and Payne, 1980).

Micromotives connote the short-term, individual self-interest side of every ethical analysis. Macrobehavior connotes the long-term implications of a decision and weighs the impact of the decision on those beyond the individual decision maker. Macrobehavior refers to what happens in the aggregate when an individual makes a decision today, and how it affects others in the future. Examining the extent to which self-interest is present in a decision helps to clarify and resolve conflicts among obligations.

A strategic ethical response is a matter of language as well as substance. The ethics of a company may be questioned simply because someone says something thoughtless when, in fact, the speaker did not mean to disregard ethical considerations. Certain phrases are dangerous, for even in casual conversation, they send a message that consideration of ethical implications are unnecessary, or extraneous, or bothersome. Dangerous phrases to watch out for are "Yes, but we've always done it that way," "Realistically . . . ," "In principle I agree, but . . . ," "Too much paperwork," "They won't do anything about it anyway," "They don't care," "They don't want to know," and "We have enough complications already."

One procedure for employers who want to highlight a renewed emphasis on ethics is to name an ethics advocate within the company. The ethics advocate is someone whose job is to raise the right ethical questions and to serve as a resource when ethical questions arise. He or she may well be someone already in the organization. This person can help set up a code of ethics and make specific proposals, such as organizing projects to ascertain the impact of a product and its moral implications. The ethics advocate should be skilled at negotiating and capable of persuading those who want to do the wrong thing to change their minds.

GUIDELINES FOR MAKING ETHICAL DECISIONS

As unique as each problem is, there is a standard set of procedures to go through to arrive at an ethical resolution. The seven steps are listed below.

1. Define the problem.
2. Acknowledge the context in which the problem arose in order to identify all stakeholders involved.
3. Identify the values that are at stake.
4. Select the values that must be maximized.
5. Choose the alternative that maximizes the essential values and minimizes as few as possible.
6. Assure that the consequences of the decision will be ethical in regard to both its short-term and its long-term consequences.
7. Implement the decision.

SUMMARY

Managers find themselves in ethical quandaries because situations are marked by multiple, noncomparable dimensions. These dimensions result from both the benefits and the harms to the organization, individuals, or the community that will result from selecting any given alternative. The problem is compounded because individuals differ on the goals, norms, beliefs, and values upon which they base their decisions.

The intuitive feeling that someone gets when coming to a decision on an ethical question is formed by what that person thinks is right, just, and fair. But when the stakes are large, such as someone's career or the moral stature and reputation of the organization, then relying on such subjective feelings is inadequate. A careful analysis of the values of caring, honesty, accountability, promise keeping, pursuit of excellence, loyalty, fairness, integrity, respect for others, and responsible citizenship is required.

Applying CHAPELFIRZ to the dilemma will lead to a careful weighing of the alternatives. The essential question to answer is not Will I do the right thing? but rather, What is the right thing to do? (Hosmer, 1988). Careful analysis of the situation, the values involved, and the consequences can bring each individual to understand what the right thing to do is. Authentic values are those by which a life can be lived and commerce can be conducted. Values only have value when they are life-enhancing. Ethical decision making is good for personal development as well as business development.

We live in a world that is not black and white. Rather, it is colored by subtle shades of gray. Situations are complex and a multiplicity of options are the rule rather than the exception. When an ethical dilemma arises, what appears to be the most obvious solution may pale as more information surfaces about the circumstances surrounding the problem. The relative priorities that people attach to different values develop over time in the context of differing situations, and are affected by friendships and life experiences.

An ethical response will never come without there being a sense of personal responsibility within those who make the decisions. Ideally, leaders in an organization will guide ethical change. However, the responsibility to *be* as an individual and act on the courage of one's convictions can sometimes be the only effective approach. Martin Buber

(1958) wrote that all living is meeting and that all relationships are mutual. He wrote: "My *Thou* affects me, as I affect it" (p. 15). To be ethical, decisions must be made in the context of the relationships that exist. This means that, as much as the courage to *be* drives individual decisions, the courage to *be* when part of a group requires more complicated decisions. More complex reasoning is required when the stakes of others are concerned in addition to one's own (Tillich, 1952).

Ethical actions on the part of employees can take two roads. One is the individual route, where one must act by oneself. The other is as part of a group. To act as an individual means ending unethical organizational behaviors by working against others. To act as a part of a group means leading an ethical organizational change by working with others and the organization (Nielsen, 1989). These approaches are not mutually exclusive, and depending on the circumstances one or both of the approaches may be appropriate for countering unethical conditions.

Bibliography

Adam, Paul J. 1963. Dealing with conflicts of interest. *Management Review* 52:50–53.

Alabama State Ethics Commission. 1983. *Advisory opinion 737.*

American Institute of Certified Public Accountants. 1989. *Code of Ethics.* New York.

Anderson, Hurst R. 1954. Ethical values in administration. *Personnel Administration* 17:1–12.

Andriacco, Dan. 1988. Ethics: The new fad in business circles spawns new business. *The Birmingham News* (July 9), p. B12.

Archer, Lawrence. 1986. The moral minority. *Canadian Business* 59:56–59.

Arrow, Kenneth J., and Herve' Raynaud. 1986. *Social choice and multicriterion decision-making.* Cambridge: MIT Press.

Association of the ICCP. 1988. *Code of ethics for certified computer professionals.* Des Plaines, IL.

Aviation Week & Space Technology. 1988. Officials warn of ethical decay in weapons buying practices. 128(June 27):20.

Baier, Kurt. 1958. *The moral point of view: A rational basis of ethics.* Ithaca: Cornell University Press.

Banner, David K., and Robert Allan Cooke. 1984. Ethical dilemmas in performance appraisal. *Journal of Business Ethics* 3:327–33.

Baram, Michael S. 1968. Trade secrets: What price loyalty? *Harvard Business Review* 46(Nov.–Dec.):66–79.

Barry, Vincent. 1979. *Moral issues in business.* Belmont, CA: Wadsworth Publishing.

Barth, Thomas J. 1987–88. Should careerists question public policy? *The Bureaucrat* 16(Winter):55–58.

Beauchamp, Tom L., and Norman E. Bowie, eds. 1979. *Ethical theory and business*. Englewood Cliffs, NJ: Prentice-Hall.

Ben-Yoav, Orly, and Dean G. Pruitt. 1984. Accountability to constituents: A two-edged sword. *Organizational Behavior and Human Performance* 34:283–95.

Birmingham Post-Herald. 1989. Air force ex-colonel is guilty of conflict (Feb. 24), p. A10.

Bloom, Allan. 1987. *The closing of the American mind*. New York: Simon and Schuster.

Bowie, Norman. 1987/88. Accountants, full disclosure, and conflicts of interest. *Business & Professional Ethics Journal* 5(3 & 4):60–73.

Bozeman, Barry. 1987. *All organizations are public: Bridging public and private organizational theories*. San Francisco: Jossey-Bass.

Brown, Thomas L. 1986a. When values collide. *Industry Week* 230(2):29–32.
———. 1986b. Bridging the value gaps. *Industry Week* 230(3):50–53.

Bruner, Robert F., and Lynn Sharp Paine. 1988. Management buyouts and managerial ethics. *California Management Review* 30(2):89–106.

Buber, Martin. 1958. *I and Thou*. New York: Charles Scribner's Sons.

Buede, Dennis M. 1986. Structuring value attributes. *Interfaces* 16(2):52–62.

Byrne, John A. 1987. Think before you blow the whistle. *Business Week* (May 18), p. 161.

Cadbury, Sir Adrian. 1987. Ethical managers make their own rules. *Harvard Business Review* 65(5):69–73.

Carson, Thomas L., Richard E. Wokutch, and Kent F. Murrmann. 1982. Bluffing in labor negotiations: Legal and ethical issues. *Journal of Business Ethics* 1:13–22.

Chalk, Rosemary. 1988. Making the world safe for whistleblowers. *Technology Review* 91(1):48–57.

Chatov, Robert. 1980. What corporate ethics statements say. *California Management Review* 22(4):20–29.

Christensen-Szalanski, Jay J. J. 1978. Problem-solving strategies: A selection mechanism, some implications, and some data. *Organizational Behavior and Human Performance* 22:307–23.

Collins, Eliza G. C. 1983. Managers and lovers. *Harvard Business Review* 61(5):144–53.

Cooke, Robert A., and Earl C. Young. 1987/88. Mergers from an ethical perspective. *Business & Professional Ethics Journal* 5(3 & 4):111–28.

Cooper, Terry L. 1986. *The responsible administrator*. Millwood, NY: Associated Faculty Press.

Cornford, Francis Macdonald, trans. 1945. *The republic of Plato*. New York: Oxford University Press.

Denhardt, Kathryn G. 1988. *The ethic of public service: Resolving moral dilemmas in public organizations.* Westport, CT: Greenwood Press.

Dittrich, John E., and Michael R. Carrell. 1979. Organizational equity perceptions, employee job satisfaction, and departmental absence and turnover rates. *Organizational Behavior and Human Performance* 24:29–40.

Donohue, John. 1988. Administrative ethics reaction paper. Unpublished manuscript.

Dozier, Janelle Brinker, and Marcia P. Miceli. 1985. Potential predictors of whistle-blowing: A prosocial behavior perspective. *Academy of Management Review* 10:823–36.

Dubinsky, Alan J., and Thomas N. Ingram. 1984. Correlates of salespeople's ethical conflict: An exploratory investigation. *Journal of Business Ethics* 3:343–53.

Ellis, Junius. 1985. Indecent exposure of your financial affairs. *Money* 14 (July):108–14

Ellison, Frederick A. 1982. Civil disobedience and whistleblowing: A comparative appraisal of two forms of dissent. *Journal of Business Ethics* 1:23–28.

Elster, Jon, ed. 1986. *Rational choice.* Washington Square: New York University Press.

ENR. 1988. Firing held discriminatory. 220(Mar. 17):14.

Erdlen, John D. 1979. Ethics and the employee relations function. *The Personnel Administrator* 24(Jan.):41–43, 68.

Ermann, M. David. 1986. How managers unintentionally encourage corporate crime. *Business and Society Review* 59(Fall):30–34.

Ferrell, O. C., and Larry G. Gresham. 1985. A contingency framework for understanding ethical decision making in marketing. *Journal of Marketing* 49(Summer):87–96.

Fisher, Cynthia D. 1978. The effects of personal control, competence, and extrinsic reward systems on intrinsic motivation. *Organizational Behavior and Human Performance* 21:273–88.

Fleishman, Joel L., and Bruce L. Payne. 1980. *Ethical dilemmas and the education of policymakers.* Hastings-on-Hudson, NY: The Hastings Center, Institute of Society, Ethics and the Life Sciences.

Frankel, Mark S. 1989. Ethics and the forensic sciences: Professional autonomy in the criminal justice system. *Journal of Forensic Sciences* 34:763–71.

Gellerman, Saul W. 1986. Why "good" managers make bad ethical choices. *Harvard Business Review* 64(4):85–90.

Hagafors, Roger, and Berndt Brehmer. 1983. Does having to justify one's judgments change the nature of the judgment process? *Organizational Behavior and Human Performance* 31:223–32.

Hanson, Kristine, and Robert Solomon. 1982. The real business ethics. *Business and Society Review* 41(Spring):58–59.

Hauserman, Nancy R. 1986. Whistle-blowing: Individual morality in a corporate society. *Business Horizons* 29(2):4–9.

Hejka-Ekins, April. 1988. Teaching ethics in public administration. *Public Administration Review* 48:885–91.

Hill, Ivan. 1981. Common sense and everyday ethics. *Security Management* 25(7):123–32.

Hornung, Mark. 1987. Honesty's valued, but transgressions abound. *Crain's Chicago Business* 10(34):1, 61–63.

Hosmer, LaRue Tone. 1988. Adding ethics to the business curriculum. *Business Horizons* 31(4):9–15.

Howard, Cecil G. 1988. Strategic guidelines for terminating employees. *The Personnel Administrator* 33(April):106–9.

Internal Revenue Service. 1986. *The commissioner's and chief counsel's annual report*. Washington, DC.

Jansen, Erik, and Mary Ann Von Glinow. 1985. Ethical ambivalence and organizational reward systems. *Academy of Management Review* 10:814–22.

Johnson, Rossall J. 1974. How second-best decisions get made. *Management Review* 63(August):30–32.

Josephson, Michael. 1988. Teaching ethical decision making and principled reasoning. *Ethics* 1(1):27–33.

Leap, Terry L., William H. Holley, Jr., and Hubert S. Feild. 1980. Equal employment opportunity and its implications for personnel practices in the 1980s. *Labor Law Journal* 31(11):669–82.

Leys, Wayne A. R. 1968. *Ethics for policy decisions: The art of asking deliberative questions*. Westport, CT: Greenwood Press.

Lindblom, Charles E. 1959. The science of "muddling through." *Public Administration Review* 19(Spring):79–88.

The Lippman report. 1987. America's disappearing ethics. Memphis: Guardsmark (Oct. 15).

Lucas, Douglas M. 1989. The ethical responsibilities of the forensic scientist: Exploring the limits. *Journal of Forensic Sciences* 34:719–29.

Lucas, Rob. 1987. Political-cultural analysis of organizations. *Academy of Management Review* 12(1):144–56.

Magner, Denise K. 1989. Students urge graduate business schools to emphasize ethical behavior and require courses in standards. *The Chronicle of Higher Education* (March 29), p. A31.

Marini, Frank, ed. 1971. *Toward a new public administration*. New York: Chandler.

Mathews, M. Cash. 1987. Whistleblowing: Acts of courage are often discouraged. *Business and Society Review* 62(Fall):40–44.

McCormick, Sheila. 1989. Whistleblowers receive consideration on Capitol Hill. *PA Times* 12(8, June 2):3.

McGowan, William. 1985. The whistleblowers hall of fame. *Business and Society Review* 52(Winter):31–36.

Miceli, Marcia Parmerlee, and Janet P. Near. 1984. The relationships among beliefs, organizational position, and whistle-blowing status: A discriminant analysis. *Academy of Management Journal* 27:687–705.

Miller, William H. 1985. A whistleblower talks: Ex-Pentagon auditor urges reforms. *Industry Week* 25(1):22–23.

Mueller, Robert K. 1977. The hidden agenda. *Harvard Business Review* 55(Sept.–Oct.):40–52.

Murphy, Patrick E. 1989. Creating ethical corporate structures. *Sloan Management Review* 30(2):81–87.

Near, Janet P. 1989. Whistle-blowing: Encourage it! *Business Horizons* 32(1): 2–6.

Nichols, Mary L., and Victoria E. Day. 1982. A comparison of moral reasoning of groups and individuals on the "defining issues test." *Academy of Management Journal* 25:201–8.

Nielsen, Richard P. 1989. Changing unethical organizational behavior. *The Academy of Management Executive* 3(2):123–30.

O'Reilly, Charles A., III, and Barton A. Weitz. 1980. Managing marginal employees: The use of warnings and dismissals. *Administrative Science Quarterly* 25:467–84.

Parmerlee, Marcia A., Janet P. Near, and Tamila C. Jansen. 1982. Correlates of whistleblowers' perceptions of organizational retaliation. *Administrative Science Quarterly* 27:17–34.

Parry, Charles W. 1985. My company—right or wrong? *Vital Speeches of the Day* 51(Aug. 1):632–34.

Pastin, Mark. 1984. Ethics as an integrating force in management. *Journal of Business Ethics* 3(4):293–304.

Paton, H. J. 1947. *The categorical imperative*. London: Hutchinson & Co.

Payne, John W., Myron L. Braunstein, and John S. Carroll. 1978. Exploring predecisional behavior: An alternative approach to decision research. *Organizational Behavior and Human Performance* 22:17–44.

Peterson, Joseph L. 1989. Symposium: Ethical conflicts in the forensic sciences. *Journal of Forensic Sciences* 34:717–18.

Price, Kenneth H. 1987. Decision responsibility, task responsibility, identifiability, and social loafing. *Organizational Behavior and Human Decision Processes* 40:330–45.

Public Management. 1987. ICMA code of ethics with guidelines. 69(8):12–13.

Ranken, Nani L. 1987/88. Conscientiousness and work roles: An individualist approach to the ethics of corporate conduct. *Business & Professional Ethics Journal* 5(1):51–68.

Rawls, John. 1971. *A theory of justice*. Cambridge: The Belknap Press.

Regazzi, John H. 1961. How to handle conflicts of interest. *The Management Review* 50(March):48–50.

Rein, Lowell G. 1980. Is your (ethical) slippage showing? *Personnel Journal* 59(Sept.):740–43.

Robin, Donald, Michael Giallourakis, Fred R. David, and Thomas E. Moritz. 1989. A different look at codes of ethics. *Business Horizons* 32(1):66–73.

Rohr, John A. 1989. *Ethics for bureaucrats: An essay on law and values*. New York: Marcel Dekker.

Ronen, Simcha. 1978. Personal values: A basis for work motivational set and work attitude. *Organizational Behavior and Human Performance* 21:80–107.

Roosevelt, Eleanor. 1940. *The moral basis of democracy*. New York: Howell, Soskin & Company.

Rose, Gerald L., Michael B. Menasco, and David J. Curry. 1982. When disagreement facilitates performance in judgment tasks: Effects of different forms of cognitive conflict, information environments, and human information processing characteristics. *Organizational Behavior and Human Performance* 29:287–306.

Roskens, Ronald W. 1988. Ethical leaders. *Vital Speeches of the Day* 54:692–95.

Rothstein, Howard G. 1986. The effects of time pressure on judgment in multiple cue probability learning. *Organizational Behavior and Human Decision Processes* 37:83–92.

Sand, Paul O. 1988. Business ethics. *Vital Speeches of the Day* 55(3):85–87.

Sanderson, Glen R., and Iris I. Varner. 1984. What's wrong with corporate codes of conduct? *Management Accounting* 66(July):28–31.

Schelling, Thomas C. 1978. *Micromotives and macrobehavior*. New York: W. W. Norton.

Schwenk, Charles R. 1984. Devil's advocacy and dialectical inquiry effects on prediction performance: Task involvement as a mediating variable. *Decision Sciences* 15:449–62.

Seymour, Sally. 1988. The case of the willful whistle-blower. *Harvard Business Review* 66(1):103–9.

Shapira, Zur, and Eli Zevulun. 1979. On the use of facet analysis in organizational behavior research: Some conceptual considerations and an example. *Organizational Behavior and Human Performance* 23:411–28.

Sheler, Jeffery L. 1981. When employees squeal on fellow workers. *U.S. News and World Report* 91(Nov. 16):81–82.

Simon, Herbert A. 1957. *Models of man*. New York: John Wiley and Sons.
———. 1976. *Administrative behavior*. New York: The Free Press.
———. 1983. *Reason in human affairs*. Berkeley, CA: Stanford University Press.
———. 1987. Rationality in psychology and economics. In *Rational Choice*, edited by Robin M. Hogarth and Melvin Warren Reder. Chicago: University of Chicago Press, pp. 25–40.
Simon, Yves R. 1986. *The definition of moral virtue*. Edited by Vukan Kuic. New York: Fordham University Press.
Smith, David R. 1986. Personal and professional responsibility. *Data Management* 24(8):6.
Smith, H. R., and Archie B. Carroll. 1984. Organizational ethics: A stacked deck. *Journal of Business Ethics* 3(2):95–100.
Solomon, Robert C., and Kristine Hanson. 1985. *It's good business*. New York: Atheneum Publishers
Stevens, Robert T. 1984. The ease of the liverwurst sandwich. *Journal of Systems Management* 35(5):42.
Taylor, Ronald N. 1975. Psychological determinants of bounded rationality: Implications for decision-making strategies. *Decision Sciences* 6:409–27.
Tillich, Paul. 1952. *The Courage to Be*. New Haven, CT: Yale University Press.
Tolchin, Martin. 1986. Investigators say it appears Deaver violated the law. *New York Times* (May 13), pp. A1, A23.
Trevino, Linda Klebe. 1986. Ethical decision making in organizations: A person-situation interactionist model. *Academy of Management Review* 11:601–17.
Tversky, Amos, and Daniel Kahneman. 1986. Rational choice and the framing of decisions. *Journal of Business* 59(4):251–78.
U.S. General Accounting Office. 1987. *Ethics enforcement: Process by which conflict of interest allegations are investigated and resolved*. Washington, DC: Government Printing Office. Report number GAO/GGD–87–83BR.
Wade, M. Euel, Jr. 1988. The lantern of ethics. *Vital Speeches of the Day* 54(11):340–43.
Walker, Susan O. 1987. Firing: Smooth and painless. *Management World* 16(6):10–12.
Wallach, Ellen J. 1983. Individuals and organizations: The cultural match. *Training and Development Journal* 37(2):29–36.
Weldon, Elizabeth, and Gina M. Gargano. 1985. Cognitive effort in additive task groups: The effects of shared responsibility on the quality of multiattribute judgments. *Organizational Behavior and Human Decision Processes* 36:348–61.

Wiener, Yoash. 1988. Forms of value systems: A focus on organizational effectiveness and cultural change and maintenance. *Academy of Management Review* 13:534–45.

Wilson, Glenn T. 1983. Solving ethical problems and saving your career. *Business Horizons* 26(6):16–20.

Wright, Donald K. 1985. Age and the moral values of practitioners. *Public Relations Review* 11(Spring):51–60.

Zumberge, James H. 1989. Ethical and moral responsibilities as faculty. *Vital Speeches of the Day* 55(7):199–202.

Index

About the Author

MARY E. GUY is Associate Professor of Political Science and Public Affairs at the University of Alabama at Birmingham. She teaches management courses in the Master's of Public Administration program and conducts research in decision processes and organization theory and behavior. Her previous books include *From Organizational Decline to Organizational Renewal: The Phoenix Syndrome* and *Professionals in Organizations: Debunking a Myth*. She has contributed chapters to books on managing human resources and has published articles in a number of journals, including *Public Administration Review, Group and Organization Studies,* and *New England Journal of Human Services*.